E.L., Saint Paul

Journeys

An Anthology of Adult Student Writing
2010

Mission:

The mission of the Minnesota Literacy Council is to share the power of learning through education, community building, and advocacy. Through this mission, MLC:

- Helps adults become self-sufficient citizens through improved literacy.
- Helps at-risk children and families gain literacy skills to increase school success.
- Strengthens communities by raising literacy levels and encouraging volunteerism.
- Raises awareness of literacy needs and services throughout the state.

Acknowledgements:

The Minnesota Literacy Council extends our heartfelt thanks to Jennifer Fierke, Jennifer Sellers and Heidi Thulin who have donated their time and their abundant creativity and talent to the planning, design, editing, and production of this book. Special thanks also to MLC staff Guy Haglund, Allison Runchey, Melissa Martinson and Cathy Grady for helping to make the book a success. Finally, we are deeply grateful for the generous donation of $500 from Todd and Mimi Burke through the Burke Family Fund in memory of Todd's late mother.

Contact Information:
The Minnesota Literacy Council
www.theMLC.org
651-645-2277
Hotline: 800-222-1990
756 Transfer Road
Saint Paul, Minnesota 55114-1404

Submissions accepted year round.

Go online to http://www.theMLC.org for Journeys Teaching & Learning Guide.

© 2010 Minnesota Literacy Council, Saint Paul, Minnesota, USA.
ISBN 13: 978-0-9844923-0-5
ISBN 10:   0-9844923-0-5

INTRODUCTION

Dear Reader,

I am happy to present the Minnesota Literacy Council's 21st annual journal of original writing and artwork by Minnesota adult literacy students. These students, who are enrolled in reading, English as a Second Language, GED, and basic skills classes across the state, have worked hard during the past year, with the help of their teachers and volunteer tutors, to be able to share their experiences with you through the written word.

The following pages contain stories by Minnesotans whose voices are rarely heard. Some are immigrants or refugees writing in their second or third language. Others are sharing their writing for the first time after years of frustration and anxiety due to their low literacy skills. All of them are improving their lives through education, often along with huge work and family responsibilities, and we are grateful that they have taken the time to share their thoughts and experiences with us.

We continue to produce Journeys year after year because we believe that it is important to our mission of sharing the power of learning. It provides a forum for the creative expression of Minnesota adult learners, a text of authentic learner stories for teachers to use in the classroom, and an acknowledgement of the tangible value and contributions of adult education to the larger Minnesota community.

During the past two decades, Journeys has grown from a thin stack of pages to a full-blown literary journal with over 400 writing and drawing submissions. We could not have done it without the hard work of our three interns, Jennifer Fierke, Jennifer Sellers and Heidi Thulin who donated hundreds of hours of their time to producing this book.

Thank you for supporting us by purchasing Journeys. I hope you enjoy it.

Sincerely,

Eric Nesheim
Executive Director

Levoy Ballard, Rochester

TABLE OF CONTENTS

Introduction	iii
Visions of Home	1
Struggles and Victories	41
Wisdom and Learning	69
Friends and Family	89
Travel and Adventure	119
Celebration and Tradition	135
Index of Authors	151

COVER ART

Front cover
To the Great Spirit
Refugio Hernández-Muniz, Elk River

Back cover
Windmill
Wilma Griebel, Southern Minnesota

Introduction - v

Randall Ringo

Visions of Home

Where I Was Born
Yuanbin Zhang, Richfield

I am from the south of China. My hometown is a beautiful small island called Hujiang. A lot of people live there. There are no cars on this island. If you go somewhere, you walk or go by boat. And one more thing, the weather is very nice. There are four seasons. Summer is not hot. Winter is not too cold, and it never snows. This is a good place to live!

Yuanbin Zhang is 27 years old and is originally from China.

Spring
Gilford Knutson, Vadnais Heights

My favorite thing to do in the spring is to walk every day in Maplewood Mall. I like to walk because it is good for my health. I enjoy going to the cabin. I like to go fishing in the boat. I like to clean and rake the yard.

Gilford Knutson is 85 years old and is originally from Canada.

Funny Story
Ka Khang, Minneapolis

When I first came to the US, I came with my husband and two children. We came to live with my husband's cousin. At nighttime, we didn't go to sleep. We stayed up all night. In the daytime, we went to sleep and my children were so hungry. I didn't know how to turn on the stove. I didn't know how to cook. And I was so shy on the phone, I didn't talk on the phone. I saw people talk on the phone and it looked like they were talking to themselves. And one month later, I wasn't shy when I talked on the phone. Now I really like to talk on the phone. I talk to my mom and my friends on the phone every night.

Now I've lived in the US for a long time. I know many things that I didn't know before. Now when I look back at my life in the past, it is very funny to me.

Ka Khang is originally from Laos.

Living in America
Amina Abdi, Minneapolis

I like living in America. I live in an apartment. I walk to this school. Sometimes I take the bus. I live with my daughter and two of her children. These are my grandchildren, too! They go to Ubah Middle School in North Minneapolis. We are happy. We play together. A house is not happy without children!

Before, I lived in Somalia. I lived in a big house. Nobody said, "Shhh!" But we had to go. Other Somali people came to my house with guns.

Now I get Social Security and medical help. I am learning English, too! God Bless all of you in America.

My First Months in America
Mostafa Guure, Minneapolis

My name is Mostafa Guure. I am from Somalia. I have lived in the United States for three months. I don't work. I have been studying at Lehmann Center for three weeks. I have five brothers and one sister. If I have free time, I like to use the Internet, watch TV, join my friends, play soccer, and help my parents every day.

I came alone to the United States. I don't have friends here, so I stay in the house. If I want to go out, I can't because I don't know this city. Sometimes, I feel I can't live here. Then everything is new for me. It is difficult, but if I study and try anything new, things will become easier. That's why I came to Lehmann Center.

My Favorite Yard
Kim Nguyen, Brooklyn Park

In my house, I have a special place. It is my yard. Every morning I go there to look at the green trees. I see the flowers opening and some yellow butterflies. They fly and sit on the flowers. I hear birds singing in the trees. I smell the green grass and I feel the fresh air.

When the winter is over and spring comes, my husband and I work in the yard. We plant flowers, tomatoes, and vegetables. We fix some places, so that they look clean and beautiful. Every weekend I go to see them grow, and I am very happy.

The yard is my favorite place, because when I am tired of hearing noises on TV, I walk around my yard. I take a deep breath of fresh air. The yard is also important for my family. My children like to play there on the weekend.

Kim Nguyen is 30 years old and is originally from Vietnam.

My First Day in Minnesota, USA
Maryan Hassan, Minneapolis

It was 2005 and my family welcomed me as a queen. They showed me my room. They said to me, "This is your room. Feel at home." I slept that night. When I woke up in the morning, I told them that I needed to get a job and needed their help. They told me they would as soon as they could but to wait a little longer. After I got my first paycheck, I remembered I wanted to go to school. Finally, I found a school and started classes. Two months later, I stopped going to school because I had a baby and also worked. Going to school was too hard for me. It is a lot of work, so that is why I still have not gotten my high school diploma.

Animals When I Was Growing Up
Nadifo Dahir, Minneapolis

This story is about animals. When I was in my country, in Somalia, I saw lots of animals like cows, goats, camels and chickens. They live in the forest. One day, my mother and I went to the forest, but I was so scared because I saw a big cow. The cow ran in front of me. I was screaming but my mother told me, "Don't be scared." Then I walked away because I knew the cow wasn't going to bite me or eat me. I am not afraid for long.

Nadifo Dahir is originally from Somalia.

My Story
Samira Mudey, Minneapolis

My name is Samira Mudey. I came from Somalia. I was born in Saudi Arabia. Now I live in Minneapolis. I have lived here for two years. I have two sons and I am also a wife. My mother and my brothers live in

Somalia. I hope one day to visit my parents and my brothers and sisters. Now I go to school five days a week for five hours a day. I take ESL classes and general education. I am not working now, but I am looking for a job. I will go to college one day to become a nurse.

The Farmer's Life in Cambodia
Chanrithy Phoung, Prior Lake

In regard to the people in my country, there are a lot of farmers—maybe 75 percent are farmers. I was born on a farm, too. In the summer time, they grow vegetables or fruits and plant rice. In the farms, there are mangoes, bananas, sugar cane, potatoes, coconuts, papayas, beans, etc.

The farmers feed animals, such as cows, buffalos, goats, chickens, and ducks to use and sell. But they couldn't make good money from their jobs, and they had no land to grow more food for their animals. In the winter, they could fish for their family and sell it. But it is cheap and doesn't give enough money, because they didn't have enough fish. They work hard, but they couldn't make more money. They could make only two or three dollars per day for their job. Many of the farmers left the country to find a job in Thailand or other countries. Some of their kids didn't go to school because they had no things to learn with, such as books, pens, pencils, rulers, erasers, etc. They need to help their parents get a job, when they are ten years old or older. The farmers are poor people in my country.

People of My Country
Anonymous, Minneapolis

People in my country are different from Americans in how they speak. My people talk with their hands—every time they talk with their hands and mouth at the same time. When Somali people are talking to each other, you think they are fighting, but they are speaking that way. I know if I go to the apartments where Somali people live, because I hear their loud voices. American people speak very quietly if they are in their house. You think their house is empty if they are close to you. You are not hearing them. When they are speaking, they are speaking only with their head.

My Country
Andja, Blaine

I am writing about my country. I was born in Croatia. It is very beautiful. I miss my family and friends a lot. I started a new life in America. I like American people, because they help me a lot at my school. They help me at my job and show me how to fill out forms.

Chinese New Year
Tiffany Eidum, Apple Valley

I am from Guangzhou, China. I have four children. I have lived in Minnesota for twelve years. I feel holidays are very different,

Wilma Griebel, Southern Minnesota

Visions of Home - 3

like New Year's Day. In America, stores are almost all closed. People are at home celebrating. But in China, if you work for a company, you have one week off. The stores are all open. The restaurants and supermarkets are all full. People like to go out to eat or go to the supermarket to buy a lot of food and cook at home with family.

Chinese New Year is a different day every year. It's usually in January, sometimes February. The first day, we stay at home with family. On the second day, we go to our parents' home to visit. On the third day, we go to our grandparents' home to visit. On the fourth day, we go to our good friends' home to visit. When you go to somebody's home, you bring some fruits and cake, put money in a small red bag, and say some good luck words to them. We give the red bags to children or old people. Then everyone is happy. I miss my country's food and friends.

My Life
Rosa Lazaro, Apple Valley

I am from Mexico. I was born in the state of Chiapas. I grew up on a farm with my parents and brothers. I have four brothers. My life on the farm was so beautiful, because my childhood home was between the mountains, a river, and a forest.

I arrived in Cancun city to find a better life with my family. I got married in Cancun. I have two children now. I lived in Cancun for nineteen years until I came to the United States with my family.

I like this country, because the school is good for learning English for my daughter and son. For me, it is difficult to speak English. I have a problem with listening. I began to work at McDonald's. This job is hard because there are many customers all day. There, I work faster and faster.

Wilma Griebel, Southern Minnesota

My Country
Taeng Chamlongsong, Minneapolis

I was born in Laos. Now I am living in the United States. Laos is a small country. In Laos, we have three seasons. They are summer, winter, and the rainy season. I like the winter season because it is not very cold like the United States, and there is no snow. In Laos, there are many holidays. My favorite is the Lao New Year. We celebrate it in the month of May. It is a very hot month of the year. Farms, offices, and businesses all are closed for one week. We eat and drink, but the main thing we do during this holiday is everybody throws water on each other. Everyone has to get wet. We do this when we get up in the morning all the way until bedtime. I miss my country a lot. I hope someday I will go back and visit. I'd love to bring my family with me. Laos is a small country, but it has a lot of beautiful things to see. We have a big, long river from north to south that's called the Maekhong River. Up north, there are mountains with different kinds of big trees and blooming flowers all year long. The air smells very fresh. In the midwest, there are mostly big cities, factories, some farmers and down to the south we have a big Niagara-like waterfall.

My Life in Laos

I grew up in Laos. We lived in a small valley. My family worked on the farm. We didn't have any bills to pay, but we didn't have any money to buy things. I remember in springtime we carried vegetables, like cucumbers, to sell at the market. Sometimes we walked to sales, carrying vegetables. We got a little money to buy soap and salt. In wintertime, we didn't have coats and shoes to wear. I was young, but I didn't go to school because my dad and my grandmother said, "You are a girl. You must stay with your mom and dad and help us."

I remember one time, my dad woke me up early in the morning—about 3:00 or 4:00—to cook breakfast for my family and prepare food for animals. We had animals, like pigs and chickens. After that, we went to work on the farm every day. We didn't know about "Saturday" and "Sunday." We didn't have a watch or clock. We just looked at the sun or moon. Every morning, we heard the roosters sound and we got up. Sometimes we worked on the farm when it was very cloudy. We didn't see the sun. We just listened for the insects' sounds—that meant evening and we came home. We didn't have a flashlight. We used oil and bamboo at night. I am very lucky—I came to the United States and changed my life. I am very happy.

Nhia Lor is a Hmong native who grew up in a small valley in Laos on her family's farm. She has been in the United States for thirteen years. She lives in Minneapolis and is currently studying English at Northside Adult Basic Education. Mai Nhia has five children, including Elena, born February 25, 2010.

Hmong Poeple

Hmong people used sickle for cutting rice stalks in the field.

White Hmong back-cask-carrying baskets in child and adult sizes

Hmong siv lub kawm no coj los mus ntim khoo thiab ntim nplej

Asian Hmong house: stool, gourd water jar, and bamboo rattan table.

This womom so only because she didn't have a family and she liked this tree so much.

Hmong people go to American from 1979, because they don't have Land and Hmongs People help America.

Pang Vang

Pang Vang, Minneapolis

My First Snow
Tao Vue, Minneapolis

My name is Tao Vue. I am from Thailand. I came to Minnesota when I was nineteen years old. Now I am 24 years old. I felt surprised when I saw snow for the first time.

One day, I looked out through the window. I saw a lot of snow on the street, cars, roofs, trees. Some children were playing and making snowmen in the front of their houses. It was very beautiful and surprised me, because I had never seen snow in my country before.

Now, the snow doesn't make me feel surprised or interested anymore because I see the snow every year in the wintertime.

My Story
Nhialue Khang, Brooklyn Park

My name is Nhialue Khang. I came from Laos. I grew up in the country of Laos. I have three brothers and three sisters. My father and mother are farmers. They don't have school in my country. They don't have electricity or telephones. When I was eight years old, I cared for yaks, goats, sheep, cows, and horses. I didn't have work shoes, pants, or a shirt. I wore only a coat. The roads were rough. The footing was too difficult.

When I was fifteen years old, I worked on a farm. We had a small farm, but the place was too high and too low. In the spring, I moved up and down. I packed my things on a black yak and horse. My older brother went to a small town. He went to driver's school for six months. He bought a new car and lived in the city. Then he moved to the city.

When I was twenty years old, I didn't have a house in the city. We lived in a small house. I rented a story. My sister went to Nepal and then to Vietnam. My sister stayed four years in Vietnam. She went back to Laos. She sent a letter to me. She wrote her address and her phone number on the letter. She found a job. She told me, "I have much money." I sent Lhasa money. "You buy a house in Lhasa," she said. I said yes. Then my brother and I went to the house she bought. It was a very big house. My brother and I are very happy too. Thank you to everyone to have special satisfaction for reading my true story.

Nhialue Khang is originally from Laos.

A Better Future
Van Le, Inver Grove Heights

My name is Van Le. I am from Vietnam and have been in the USA for three months. In the USA, everything is very difficult and different for me. I don't speak English and I don't drive a car. I still remember about my country. In that I had been with my brothers, my sisters, and my friends. I lived in Vietnam merrier and happier. The first day in the New Year, we get together so that we eat and drink very much. We sing and play music until midnight. Now I live in the USA because I want my children to go to school here. It has been very difficult but we will stay for our better future. I want to learn English and work very nice. I hope someday I will have more money and visit my country.

Van Le is originally from Vietnam.

Coming to America
Aung Kyaing, Saint Paul

My name is Aung Kyaing. I am from Nupho Refugee Camp, Thailand. My mother and my father live in Burma. I had five brothers. My first brother and four young brothers lived with my mother in Burma. Four of them are dead. My father is dead. My third young brother lives in Canada. My family and I came to Thailand. My family and I lived in a little house in the Nupho Refugee Camp. In Thailand, my family and I made Burma and Karen clothes. We ate rice and peppers and eggs, fish, pork and red onions and vegetables. I married in Burma. I have seven children. The first six were born in the forest in Burma. The seventh was born in the refugee camp. They are ages 32 to eight. Our children were born at home in the forest, because the forest has no hospital.

My family and I decided to come to America. On February 17, 2009 at 7 a.m., we took the bus to the airport to America. I stayed home two months. After two months, I went to school in LEAP. I like to study English and I don't like snow. My fifth child goes to school in LEAP high school. She is in tenth grade. My sixth child goes to school in Washington Technology Magnet Middle School. She is in eighth grade. My seventh child goes to school in Mississippi Creative Art Magnet School. She is in second grade. My first, second and fourth go to jobs and the third child has no job. In America, my family is living in a good house with three bedrooms and one big bedroom. My daughter pays the money every month. My family is very happy, and I am happy too.

I miss my mother, and in Burma, my mother misses me.

Aung Kyaing is originally from Burma.

My Life Story
Daniel Lemu, Apple Valley

I came from Ethiopia on June 20, 2005. I am married. My wife and I have been married for 15 years. We have two children, one boy and one girl. My son is 13 years old. He is in the seventh grade. My daughter is five years old. She is in kindergarten.

I have been working at Ray Way Industrial for four years. My life is better than when I lived in Ethiopia. In Ethiopia, I was a construction worker. I was a hard worker, but my life was good. I didn't earn enough money, so I changed my idea. That is how I made my own business. I made all kinds of bricks, like wall bricks, big concrete bricks, and concrete tubes. I made the concrete tubes and bricks by using a machine that I made. While I was making the bricks, I got the chance to come to the United States with my family. The business I had was good. But coming here was better. Now my life is better in the United States. The reason I came here was to get a better job and education for me and for my family.

Daniel Lemu is originally from Ethiopia.

My Life in America
Anonymous, Apple Valley

I am from Burma. I arrived in the U.S. on July 15th, 2008 as a refugee. Now I am living in Farmington and working at the Thai restaurant in Apple Valley. I also go to Grace Adult School in the morning for ESL classes. It's a nice school and the teaching system is really good. Students are from different countries and speak different languages. I like to study in the US because it's a really different educational system from my country. I want to be a nursing assistant in the future.

I don't like winter in Minnesota. When we go somewhere, we need a car or bus because of snow. My country has lovely weather and the trees are always green and there's no snow. We can go anywhere without a car or bus. Sometimes I call my parents and we talk about my life in America.

My House
Carrie White, Duluth

I live in front of Lake Superior. Years ago, the house that I live in used to be closer to Lake Superior. They moved the house closer to the road so that Lake Superior wouldn't flood it. Before it was moved, it was a trading post for the Army. After it was moved it was called the Depot. It was a restaurant. It is interesting that the house is sitting on an Indian burial ground.

Today we call it the Depot House. It is an adult foster home for people who have brain injuries. We will be able to live out in the community once we are doing better. We will be on our own in the community.

The house has a lot of history, and the house has changed over the years. We are changing too. The house is yellow and brown. It is close to Jay Cooke Park and Fond-du-lac camping too.

Time
Anonymous, Edina

My family and I came to the USA almost three months ago. At first, I was very sad, because I missed everything—my friends, my cat, my house, my mother-in-law, and my job. Also, I didn't speak English. But now, I am happy to be here in Minneapolis, because I enjoy the time with my children. My sister and I have time to share. She has been married for nineteen years. My brother-in-law and my nephews and I are very close. It's a great time for us. In my country, I had a good job, but I had to work too many hours every day. I never had enough time to enjoy anything. I felt I lost many fun things.

I listened to my daughter speak. She is three years old. It is very fun to see how my daughter sees the world. Every day, she tells me some stories about how the things have to be. One time, she said to her teacher, "My mom has gone to the school to learn English. I am smart, because I speak English already. I can play with other children." She is adorable. I thought about that, and she is right. We are smart people, but we have too much to do here.

I have to find a part-time job, because we need money. Well, everybody needs money, but I don't want to change my time with my children. They are growing up very fast, and someday they will not need me anymore. I am thinking nothing is perfect—just the time to enjoy things.

My Life in My Old Country
Soua Thao, Minneapolis

When I was in my old country, I lived with my family. It was a big family. I'm the middle child of my family. I have seven brothers and four sisters. We lived in a large house together in a small town in the North of Laos. When I was a kid, I walked to school with my sisters and my brothers. It took about thirty minutes. Then we hurried. We ran to school, because our school was far from my house. In the evening, I went to water my garden. Every Saturday and Sunday, we went to help our parents work on the farm to plant rice, corn, vegetables and many things to feed animals. In my free time, I liked to go fishing and swimming in the river. I also went to hike in the mountains and to pick fruit from the forest with my friends.

> I am happy to be here in Minneapolis, because I enjoy the time with my children.

During the time I was a teenager, I didn't have a job to earn money. I only studied and planted vegetables, corn and cucumbers in my garden and we owned domestic farm animals to sell to earn money. We didn't have a car or truck. I only rode a bicycle. We used a cart and a horse to transport our crops home. We used a water buffalo to plow the soil and harrow the rice field. In a year, we could plant rice and have two harvests.

Even though my life in Laos was difficult and we worked hard on the farm, we also had a lot of fun and joy with my friends and my family.

My First Time in an Airplane
Denise Agbenowossi, Minneapolis

I'm from Togo, a small country in West Africa. Togo is a poor country, but in the city, lots of people have the opportunity to buy a TV, a freezer, or a refrigerator—even a car. I was one of those people.

When I came to the USA, I saw every single person has all these things, and I was surprised. I don't have to wash my clothes with my hands or dry them with sunshine like in my hometown. I can use the laundry and pay. That's wonderful. But my favorite is the microwave. It is so easy and so fast. I like using it. I hope I'll get one and send it to my parents, so they can enjoy it.

A Wonderful Life
Chan Hou, West Saint Paul

My name is Chan Hou. I'm from Cambodia. I was born on November 1st, 1970. I was born in Phnom Penh, Cambodia. I came to the United States in 2004. When I came for the first time, I thought, "This country is very big and beautiful." Before, I never, never thought I would be in this country. But for me it was very hard to live with my friend, my job, my life and all, especially since I can't speak English. I didn't have a job, money or a driver's license. My wife worked in nutrition in a nursing home in West Saint Paul. My wife taught me driving. We decided to get married in 2004. I got a job in 2006 at Tyco Plastics. I worked over there for three years. My company was closed. I became a US citizen in 2007. My counselor helped me go to college. On September 11th, 2009 I got a license for nursing assistant. I'm going to look for a job in February 2010.

When I came to Minnesota, the first time I saw snow was November 10th, 2004. My country has no snow. Every time I see the snow I'm scared. I don't like it. Some people live in Minnesota a long time. They like the snow, and some people who have farms like the snow because their farms depend on the snow. If they don't have the snow, they complain all the time and say, "What's wrong with the snow this year?"

Today, I sat the whole day in front of the TV to see the inauguration of Barack Obama, President of the United States. I could understand the English. People can get lots of facilities for study in the US.

I've met more people from different countries. If I hadn't come to the US, I couldn't know or even think about these wonderful people here. I like Minnesota because the lakes are beautiful, but I don't like the cold. For me it was very hard. I go to school from Monday to Thursday morning. I come home at 11:30. Now I don't have a job but I like learning and I'm happy. I love my wife and my son, so I have a wonderful life.

Chan Hou is originally from Cambodia.

Forgotten
David Boggie, Ogilvie

Forget the day as it is,
Forget the reason I make this list,
Forget the people in my head,
Forget the bitching in the line ahead,
Forget the reason that brought me here,
Forget the things I once had feared,
Forget all the things I dread in hopes,
To make room for what lies ahead instead.

Cinquain
Jonathon Smith, Duluth

Missing in time of need
No one understands me
Alone it seems
Serenity breached
Freak

Jonathon Smith is 23 years old and is originally from California.

Poem for Barack Obama
Mohamed Warsame, Minneapolis

Barack Obama, the people of America have chosen you and God has given you a chance.
Your knowledge and your wisdom will make your job easier for you.
God will help you with your decisions.
People are looking to you, for the promises you made.
I am praying for you, for your safety and protection.
I am praying for your lifelong happiness.
I am praying that you accomplish your goals.
I am praying to Allah that the people will trust you.
I am praying that God gives you health and strength to do what is deemed necessary.
I am praying to Allah that you have no enemies.
I am praying to God for your long life and health.
I am praying that Allah makes America a better place for all.
I am praying to God that the people will allow you another four years in the White House.
I am praying to Allah that all people—of all religions—will trust you and help you make peace for everyone.

Mohamed Warsame is 50 years old and is originally from Somalia.

Untitled
Bernardino Enríquez, Saint Paul

I helped my parents. When I was eleven or twelve years old in my town, I helped my parents to work in the field. They had animals. I took care of the goats, lambs, horses, and cows. Sometimes, my father had to sell some animals for money to buy clothes, shoes, fruit, food, and everything. In 1980, I went to Mexico City. I worked in a restaurant in the Gate C airport for five years. After that, I worked in the downtown city for fourteen years as a waiter in the restaurant Hotel Majestic. I always helped my family. Six years ago, I came to the US. I arrived in the airport of Minneapolis. I'm an English student in the winter. Sometimes, I understand a little bit, and sometimes I do not understand anything, but I try to learn. Learning as an adult is more difficult than learning as a boy. My family needs help. I have to send money often. It is necessary for them.

Bernardino Enríquez is originally from Oaxaca, Mexico.

Untitled
Sadia I., Saint Louis Park

When I came to America, it was the beginning of Fall. Everything was green for awhile, and then everything changed green to yellow, orange and red. All the leaves started to fall down, and all the trees looked like they were dead. I was amazed how this process changed from the beginning to the end. My family told me this is the end of Fall and the beginning of winter. I was looking forward to seeing snow for the fist time in my life. When I saw the snow, I was every excited. I even went outside to feel and touch it. It was so beautiful. The sky was cloudy and all trees were full of snow. Though people complain about driving, it is gorgeous to me. We don't have this kind of weather in Somalia. Fall change leaves and falling snow. I was so excited by this weather.

All Is Possible!
Cenovia Lagunas, Marshall

I came to the USA in 1980, but I had only one year here. I went back to my country because I was pregnant, and my husband and I did not have a job. My oldest daughter was born in Mexico. Then we came again to the USA. We had no papers. It was hard, because again we didn't have a job, and I was pregnant a second time. My husband sent me to Mexico again, and my second daughter was born in Mexico too. It was hard, because we didn't speak English. We lived in California. In California, we did not need to speak much English. But when I came to Minnesota, I needed an interpreter with me every place and for everything. It was hard, but now I am better, because I am learning English and I have my citizenship.

Cenovia Lagunas is 48 years old and is originally from Mexico.

Life in Minnesota
Melia Yang, Saint Paul

Minnesota is a big state. It is beautiful. It has 10,000 lakes. Many people like going fishing. It also has four seasons and larger malls for shopping. My family lives in Minnesota. In the summer time, we like to go fishing, run around the lake, and BBQ outside. In the summer time, all the leaves turn to green. Minnesota is a good place to live.

Melia Yang is originally from Laos.

Americans Are Friendly
Orathai (Wai), Owatonna

I've been in the USA for awhile. I've learned many things from here and have had good and bad experiences. However, I choose to memorize only the good things.

As a new arrival in Minnesota, I didn't have any friends or someone else who I knew besides my host family. I noticed that people say "Hi" to each other and me. One day, I stood in front of my house, when an old man and an old woman sitting next to him drove past me and opened the window to say hi to me. I was confused a bit. I didn't know them. "They were very friendly," I thought in my mind, I will always remember them. Now I always greet them when I see them and the others who I walk past on the street. It makes me feel happy!

Orathai (Wai) is originally from Bangkok, Thailand.

A Nice Town
Abdinasir Aden, Minneapolis

When I lived in southern Somalia, I lived in Kismayo. That town is a very beautiful and sunny beach town. It is very nice and the weather is better than in Minneapolis. It is a good place to live and has everything that you need. There is no snow and no cold and you don't fear anything. You have everything you need, because you stay in your own house, in your own country, which costs nothing. In Somalia you have restaurants and tea shops of your own and all the people know you very well because they are your neighbors. You and they were born in one place and one town and all people are your friends. You can go everywhere you need to in the town. You can play football, watch TV, and go to tea shops. But here it is not like that. Here all the people are busy. That is why it is different here and that is why I like my country and my nice town in Somalia.

Celebrating the New Year
Wah Eh, Saint Paul

Every year on January first, we celebrate the Karen New Year. All people wear Karen clothes. Some people come from different countries, so they can wear their clothes. We have some food for the guests, like fruit and tea. Our Karen people usually eat sticky rice and dry fish, because it came from a long time ago, from our parents and grandparents. We use this day for our memories. Ever year on New Year's Day, we celebrate like our parents and grandparents did before. We give gifts to our friends too.

The Place I Was Born
Pa Lor, Saint Paul

The place I was born was a small village, but it was very flat and a good place to live. It was a very safe place for people, because there were no thieves or robbers. People were also friendly and helped each other plant seeds and grow food.

When I was a child, I very much liked to follow my mom and dad to the farm. I also liked to help them raise animals—I especially liked chickens, pigs and horses. I fed them every morning, and I used to ride a horse when I was young.

Sometimes, I went with my older brother to the jungle or forest to hunt birds or squirrels. He used a cross bow to kill them. Sometimes he used a basket to trap the birds or squirrels. My brother knew how to swim very well, and he liked to use the cross bow to hunt fish under the water or rocks. Sometimes, he used a fish net to catch first. I liked to go with him.

When I was in class or school, I liked to read, write and listen to the teacher. After school, I liked to play with my friends or classmates. We jumped rope and played with small rocks on the soil.

When I was young, my hobbies were playing soccer, planting flowers, gardening, and sometimes playing with my little sister. When I played with my little sister, I didn't think about anything else and we had fun together. I like to plant flowers because I wanted my house full of flowers that were beautiful. Around my house were flowers and I enjoyed it very much. I planted a garden in my back yard and I planted papaya trees and banana trees too.

That was my wonderful world.

Pa Lor is originally from Laos.

The Dream of a Little Chinese Girl
Hui Luo, Prior Lake

My name is Hui Luo. I come from southern China. I was living in Nanning which is a city that never has snow in the winter. When I was a little girl, I saw some beautiful women from northern China. I was dreaming about if I could move to the north. Then I would be a gorgeous lady like one of them after I grew up.

In 2008, I married and moved to Minnesota in the US. It's in the northern part of the US, of course the north of the earth too. The lowest temperature can be -40 degrees Fahrenheit in the winter. You can imagine how freezing cold it is. Sometimes, I doubted whether my dream was right, but after I survived the first winter, I knew I had to and must get used to the cold. Anyway, Minnesota is a beautiful state with nice people, isn't it? I think my dream came true. I will enrich myself and gain more and more beauty inside.

Vang Hang, Sartell

My New Life in the U.S.
Israel Zamorano, Minneapolis

My name is Israel and I am from Morelos, Mexico. I came to the United States three years ago. My brother, Juan, is here. He is married to Maria and they have two boys, but my mom and dad and my five brothers all live in Mexico.

I work full time in a factory—Specialty Food. I can do several jobs at this factory. Sometimes, I do different things like cleaning the machines; at other times, I'm a machine operator.

In my free time, I listen to music. I like all types of music, but especially romantic music. On Saturday night, I play soccer with my friends from work. Right now, I'm studying English.

From Somalia to Minnesota
Fatuma Hirsi, Apple Valley

When I was in my country, I was a student. But at that time, a civil war broke out, so we ran to Kenya. In 1991, I went from Somalia to Kenya. Life there was not how I was living in my country. Sometimes it was harsh. Sometimes it was good. Then in 2001, I moved to America. The first time I came to America, there was a bit of snow and cold, but it was okay because I knew it was cold. At that time, I was feeling very happy.

I live with my husband and my children. I have a good life. In America, the American people are friendly, especially Minnesota people. Sometimes they ask me some things, like about how I dress, but I give them good answers. Life is good and I feel very happy!

> The American people are friendly, especially Minnesota people. Sometimes they ask me some things, like about how I dress, but I give them good answers. Life is good and I feel very happy!

America Is Good and Bad
Aregash Gemedi, Minneapolis

I live in South Minneapolis. I like to clean my home and I always like to cook. I make enjara and many other foods for my family. I have a husband. He is losing his memory. Our doctor helps him. We have fourteen children. Eight children live in Minneapolis. Six children are near Seshomenee, Ethiopia.

Life is hard here too, and we are not safe. I speak Oromo. Communicating is not easy. The shooting and car accidents are not good. The stress of not having a job is also not good. There are some jobs too hard for anybody. I think about my country and my children every day.

I do like America! American people have done many good things for us. We get help at the hospital when we are sick. I learn English at Volunteers of America Adult High School. We also get food stamps to buy strawberries, bananas, onions, carrots, pasta, teff and all we need. We have problems, but we are very, very glad to be here.

My Quiet Place...
Robert A. Smith, Elk River

Is a night's fishing trip on Lake Waverly. Sunsets are an orange glow over the horizon. The waves seem to slow down to a flat glasslike stillness as night falls. I load my boat with the necessary supplies and head to the center of the lake. Dropping anchor, I hear the sound of a distant loon calling to another. I just sit and forget all my day's problems and wait for the first bite.

Visions of Home - 15

Memory of My Little Home Town

I lived in a small, quiet town as a child and throughout my teenage life. I used to swim in lakes with other kids. Sometimes we made traps from wood and caught rabbits and turkeys. Usually we had meals two times a day. When we decided to play outside for a whole day, we used to eat peanuts and drink from the river. One day, a boy read a story to me and showed me a picture he had drawn. I was very impressed, and I fell in love with school. But the distance of the school from where I lived kept me away for a long time. The nearest one was 15 miles away, and I was 9 years old. My parents wouldn't let me walk that far. I begged my brothers to teach me.

At the age of 15, I decided to pursue my educational ambition on my own. I walked into the school office for registration, and they asked me for transcripts. I didn't have any. They said I was too old to be placed in first grade. I told them I had some basic education and pleaded with them to give me a chance. They gave me a test and placed me in fifth grade. I began walking about 30 miles to and from school every day until cold weather came. Then it became difficult for me.

My father died when I was 13, and I had to go to one of my father's best friends who had horses, and I asked him for one. He gave me one. He said to get someone who would train both of you, or you will be harmed and I'll be embarrassed. I couldn't find anyone who would train me. I tried for a couple days. Then I rode to the school. When I arrived in the city, my horse reacted to the noise and was startled, and I lost control of it. While I was in chaos, my classmates were cheering me on. Later, when I told them I was scared, they laughed. I continued chasing my dream until it was disrupted by civil war. Thanks to the USA, today my kids and I are learning with terrific treatment. One day, I must take my kids back home to witness for myself how kids are attending school over there and living their daily lives. So then my kids can appreciate this wonderful country more.

Naji Ibrahim has been a Level 6 student at the Lehmann Center for only a few months but will already be moving to the Transitions class soon. He was born in Somalia and grew up in Ethiopia, but left when the civil war broke out. He has lived in the U.S. for 15 years and has had a variety of jobs, from taxi driver to grocery store owner. Now he hopes to get his GED, attend college, and find a career in a medical field. He lives in Minneapolis and has three children.

My Dream
Johan Cerra, Minneapolis

I have a dream that one day I will live in freedom with all the world.
I have a dream that someday my family will live in freedom with me.
I have a dream that one day this country will open the arms for all the people there.
I have a dream that one day all people in the word will live in freedom and be happy and dream like me.

Johan Cerra is 55 years old and is originally from Santiago de Cuba.

Raising Sheep in Minnesota
Bill Gaskin, Red Wing

I was raised on a farm near Rochester, Minnesota. I was active in 4-H, becoming president for one year.

I raised sheep and enjoyed it because I didn't need any expensive equipment. To raise sheep, I would start out with 25 ewes. Take time to get advice and read up on sheep-raising before you start. They are a two-income livestock, meat and wool. You must realize they are not just for eating weeds and grass, if you want to make money.

Choose ewes with long bodies, straight legs, and a sound milk bag. I would not start out with ewe lambs as they would be more troublesome than mature ewes because ewe lambs need more help lambing. If you aren't cautious, you might cut her uterus, and she will bleed to death. However, when choosing mature ewes, be sure they have all their teeth. Sicknesses such as mastitis can be fatal to a lamb sucking such a ewe. A long body is beneficial for the ewes to carry multiple lambs. The male or ram on the other hand, should be short bodied, deep-chested and straight-legged. I don't know if it's true or not, but when I was raising them, we wanted twin lambs because one provided the cost of boarding a ewe, and the other one was your profit. The gestation period averages out to be about 145 days. Start out by having late spring lambs because they are easier to care for. Most breeds will not come into heat until we have a frost. Approximately 15 days before breeding, you should feed the ewes one-third pound of grain a day to increase chances of multiple birth. You should feed them a high-protein hay. They eat approximately three pounds of hay a day.

Before or after the ewes give birth, you should sheer your sheep. Wool is not very profitable. Black-face sheep would not usually have as much wool as white-faced sheep. The pasture is usually at its best in June. You can get your May lambs off to a good start. It takes about five or six months to get them to market weight, or 100 to 120 pounds.

Take time to get advice and read up on sheep-raising before you start. Sheep can be very loveable. I hope you have fun raising them!

What I Love, What I Miss
Anonymous, Minneapolis

I came from Vietnam in June 2008. I am living with my husband in Minneapolis, Minnesota. I like the winter and autumn, because snow is beautiful. It is bright like diamonds. Even though winter is very cold, I walk every day from home to school. I enjoy walking outside very much, so I can see the snow near to me. When I was young, I saw many foreign country movies. I wished I could see real snow. Today it came true, so I like winter and I also like autumn. Autumn is beautiful too. The leaves change color from green to yellow. When I wake up in the morning, I see through the window that, day by day, the leaves clearly changed. It seems to be very magical and strange to me. The only thing I miss is my parents. I am the youngest in my family, and I was very close to them. It was nearly 34 years ago, and I never went far from them until I married. I remember when the Lunar New Year came, my parents and I cleaned the house. Sometimes the paint came off the wall, and we painted it for Lunar New Year. At the beginning of New Year, we went to the pagoda to pay blessings to Buddha for our family's happiness and peace.

My Belorussian Roots
Vadim, Coon Rapids

My name is Vadim. I am from Belarus, a country in the middle of Europe. Three things that I like about my country are food, religion and history. First, religion is a big part of my life and my family. My religion is very old and came to me from my parents. I would like to teach that to my children too. Second, traditional food is very important. I'd like to cook for my friends and my family. Third, the history of my country is very important. I like my country which has thousands of years of history. I like the city in which I was born. It's the capital of Belarus and a very beautiful city. I want to teach my children these important things about my culture.

A Snow Blower
Yong Hong Zhu, Owatonna

I like to see the snow through the window. So when the snow was coming, I was so excited. However, my husband always gets a headache about this snow, because he knows he will have a hard job to do. He wanted to buy a snow blower; I did not agree and I thought shoveling snow is a good exercise for the body. Another reason is a snow blower is expensive and it is rarely used. The last reason is I think shoveling snow is very fun.

During this Christmas holiday, we had a big snowstorm. When I was shoveling snow, I found out it was a very hard job. I realized it was a harder job than what I thought. I now know why my husband complained about snow shoveling.

We are happy right now because we bought a snow blower. We never worry about when snow is coming.

Yong Hong Zhu is 38 years old and is originally from China.

Differences in America
Hong Le, Lakeville

I am from Vietnam. I was born in Vietnam. My village has a beautiful lake and a lot of trees. I came to America to join my husband almost two years ago. He is a good man. I had my first child here.

Since I arrived in the US two years ago, I think America is different from my country. The people in America come from around the world and speak different languages. America has a different climate than my country. My country is rainy and sunny almost the whole year. The winter in America is so long, but summer is great in Minnesota.

One thing made me surprised: The vehicles in America are very easy to drive. The vehicles in Vietnam all go on the same road. The cars, bikes, and motorcycles all go together. Here, they go separately.

> One thing made me surprised: The vehicles in America are very easy to drive.

My Wife and I
Toua Her, Brooklyn Center

I came to America on March 19, 2008. It is very exciting for me, because it is my first time seeing snow and cold weather. On the other hand, there are many tall buildings and a lot of traffic. I like the USA, but everything is difficult for me, because we are new people in America. But I can study English, and I can learn American culture. I must, for my dream.

I love my country, Laos. During the time I lived in Laos, I enjoyed being with my friends very much, because we hardly ever went to Vang Vieng. Vang Vieng is the most beautiful place in Laos. It has many high mountains, caves and clear rivers. We took pictures of each other. Those are my memories. I hope I will be going to visit my home country, Laos, in the next couple years.

Coping with Winter in Minnesota
Abdullahi Farah, Minneapolis

Minnesota is very bad in wintertime. I'm so unhappy. Most people complain about severe weather. I am very careful when I drive my car. I don't like when snow falls down on land. After one day it is slippery. When I came to Minnesota, I saw a lot of snow on the ground. The United States has different weather and culture. But something is similar. I think this country is bigger than my country. American people are good people and work hard. I was very happy when I came to the airport and went home. I was very excited to see my relatives again.

Abdullahi Farah is originally from Somalia.

My Arrival in the United States
Leyla Aden, Minneapolis

I was more than happy to come to the United States. All I was feeling was happiness for my new life, but when I arrived here I felt homesick, and I started crying. The people who were welcoming me thought that I was crying because I had missed them. But my situation was different from what they thought. By the time I arrived, I started remembering my family. I felt lonely and I couldn't sleep day or night. It was horrible for me. I didn't know what to do or who to talk to. I got confused and frustrated. I couldn't call my family because I didn't have money to buy a calling card, but even if I did it wouldn't give me enough minutes to talk to my whole family. Whenever I talked to them, I got more homesick. The nights got longer and I was full of anxiety. Every time I tried to sleep, I remembered my mother and my siblings.

Besides the homesickness, I couldn't stand the new climate. The country I come from is hot, but here I had to wear a jacket and sweater and I couldn't get used to those things. It was amazing for me, because I didn't know how to survive the cold weather. I'd never seen snow and I didn't know how to buy the proper clothes. Sometimes I wore only a light sweater when it was pretty cold outside. One day, I went outside in slippers and it was snowing. It took awhile to learn my lesson, but now I am used to the cold climate.

In addition, I had culture shock when I came to the US. Everything was different from my culture. I was used to an environment where everyone covered his or her body, but here it is totally different. People are free to do whatever they want to. They can cover their body or not. No one forces them to do anything. They have the freedom and the choice. In my country, kids are not free even if they are 18 years old. They have to live with their parents until they get married.

Everything was different from what I thought. I came to a new country that is totally different from my country. I was frustrated because of the climate, the homesickness and the culture shock.

Coming to the USA
Sokunthea Hean, Burnsville

I miss my friends and my family in Cambodia. I have three brothers. In Cambodia, my life was like a princess because my parents had only one girl—me. In Cambodia, I went to study, went shopping, and sometimes went for walks with my friends. Especially I miss my country's New Year. It was a happy time with my family. We went to a province in my country.

When I came to the USA, my life changed. I needed to do everything by myself. I needed to improve my English because my English was poor. I needed to find a job to earn money by myself.

Before, I didn't like it here so much, but now I'm starting to love this country as much as I can, because here I learn how to be an independent person and be stronger than before.

A Happy-Go-Lucky Lonely Man
Abdullahi Hersi, Oakdale

I was born in Somalia in 1983. I was a student most of the time. When I came home from school, I helped my parents, because they had a small business. In my free time, I played soccer in my district. I was definitely so happy.

One day, I decided to go to Ethiopia. I made a process for a visa to America. After a couple of years, I got the visa and came to America. I felt so lonely. I saw different life, different people, and different cultures. I was happy to see all that. I am a happy-go-lucky man, yet, I sometimes feel lonely.

Abdullahi Hersi is 25 years old and is originally from Somalia.

My Country
Brenda Franco, West Saint Paul

My name is Brenda. I am from Nuevo Laredo, Tamaolipas, Mexico. I like my country very much. I like to eat beef tacos and like to go on long walks to the park and eat very spicy hot corn. In my family every weekend we have a barbecue. I miss my family very much and my country too.

The Snow
Adam Dhunkal, Minneapolis

Last night there was blizzard weather over most of the Midwest. The weatherman said, "Mother Nature dropped between seven and nine inches of snow and 30 mile per hour winds in 12 hours." In the morning, there was a heap of snow all around our house. At 8 o'clock, I took my shovel, and I plowed all the way around my house. When I was in Africa, I had never experienced snow. All we know about snow was what we used to see on the TV or read in newspapers and magazines, but I always used to imagine when it snowed on you the snow could be as heavy

> I always used to imagine when it snowed on you the snow could be as heavy as raindrops.

as raindrops. Surprisingly, the snowflakes are very, very light. You can hardly feel them.

Funny Story
Zahra Mohammed, Minneapolis

When I came to the United States, I decided to go to school, but I didn't know how to go to school and I didn't have a car. I asked a woman how I could go to school. She told me that I could catch the bus. I didn't know which bus to ride.

One day, I saw a school bus drop kids in front of my building. I went into the bus because I thought that everybody going to school could ride the school bus. When I got in the bus, the driver shouted. He said to me, "Go out, please!"

I told him that I was going to school. The driver was confused, and he couldn't close the bus's door because I was in the bus. Finally, a woman who lived in my building saw me and told me that this school bus did not take adult people to school. I had to go out and catch a city bus.

After that, any time I remember about that story, I just laugh. Because it was the funniest story I had in my entire life. Whenever I tell somebody about this story, they all laugh too.

Zahra Mohammed is 35 years old and is originally from Somalia.

My Second Home
Jian Zou (Amy), Ramsey

My name is Amy, and I'm from China. I was born in a beautiful seaside city, Dalian. With loving parents, we grew up as a family. I had lived more than 30 years of life. Never did I think my life would change. I met my husband because he came to work in Shanghai, China. He is a kind person that likes the people, scenery, and delicious food in China.

We both love China but also wanted our daughter to have a good school for learning, so we left our home in China and went to the USA. We had lived in Shanghai for many years waiting for our home in the United States. I came to the USA one year ago. I'm really homesick and miss my family (parents, brother, sister and the baby we were raising) who now seem like strangers to me. All is in place to start a new life, but this life is very difficult for me. Everything must start from scratch. Learning a new language is my top goal so I attend night school to learn the English language from great teachers to be ready for a new occupation. Being happy can also be found in work if that's what you want.

The pace of life here is very fast. The pressure to change is great. I want to quickly adapt to my new home, to settle down and have a good life, but mostly to build our second happy home like I had in China.

Village of Dong Ang, Fu Jiang State, China
Feicui Liu, Elk River

I have a quiet place. It's a flat roof of my house in my little village. I lived in my village until I needed to go to school in the city. I love my quiet place, so every morning I would go there to take a look, breathe fresh air and relax.

There, it is very quiet and is a little high up. You can see some houses all around and then the mountains after the houses. There is a lot of green, also some fruit trees and different kinds of flowers in the mountains. It is very beautiful!

Look in the distance. There is a big river between two islands, so you can also see another island view.

I think you would like my quiet place,

because you can see little houses, little roads, green mountains, a blue river, little islands and clear sky all at one time.

Survival Traditions
Anonymous, Hopkins

In Somalia, there are some traditional ways to live. These ways include farmers, those who live in the city, and nomads. It can be very rough living to some people, but it has its good side in addition to its bad side.

Most Somali people are farmers. It's good to have a farm when you have a big family. If you have a big family, the family members can help in many ways. Some can help plant the corn, and when the corn is ready, they can export it to the big cities and make big money. But of course, also you have to have a good season to grow. Farmers sometimes starve to death because of lack of rain. When it's bad like that, people depend on the money they make by exporting grains.

The other group lives in the city; they have shops and work in the city. They also depend on farmers, because the food they sell and eat is grown by somebody else. They also import sugar, oil, clothing, and any other things that they could make a profit by selling to the shoppers.

There are also the nomads who live in the country with their livestock. They move from place to place. They follow the seasons. They move a lot and go wherever they can find something their animals could eat. They have animals like cows, camels, goats, sheep, and donkeys. It's hard living the nomads' life, but when you adopt it, it's easier than it looks. There are lower and higher places in Somalia. In the summer they go into the lower places where it's cooler than in high places. The lower places have rivers and lakes, but when the rainy season begins, they have to move to higher places, otherwise their animals would die. If you stay in the lower places, there is some kind of ant that comes out in the rainy season and kills a lot of animals.

It can be pretty rough living in Somalia, but it's a lot of fun. People there are healthy. You don't have to exercise for the rest of your life because we mostly walk and most of the daily routine involves walking a long distance.

A Farmer Culture in Sudan
Aisha Adam Mahmoud, Minneapolis

Every country has different culture and tradition. In my country, Sudan, there are many tribes and languages, but everybody speaks Arabic. It is some of the farmers' culture. They are living outside of the city, about two or three days away from the city. They come to the city just when they want some stuff and to buy what they need for a month, because it is hard for them to come every week. And they own camel, sheep, goats, and chickens. And they support the city with that.

They don't allow their kids to go to school or go to the city, because their kids take care of the animals when they become six or seven years old. They live in one big room—all the family together. And when their daughter or son turns 9 years old they should get a marriage very soon. And the family takes care of them after they get married until they get babies. These people move from place to another to take care of the animals, looking for food and water.

When I Came to the USA
Marian Firin, Minneapolis

When I first came to the United States, I thought when people wanted to rent a house, the house would include furniture. But I was wrong, because when I rented my first house I had to buy everything I needed.

The second thing that surprised me when I

first came to the United States was wintertime. When I came, it was cold and snowy. I was surprised, because I didn't know about snow, but I understood it within a few days. I felt very cold, but I was OK. I miss my country's weather, because it has good weather.

I remember the first day I took the bus. My brother gave me directions and I took the bus, but I felt very afraid. Another day, I took the bus again, but I got lost and couldn't find my home. I was scared when I was lost, but I got home a few hours later and I felt happy when I got home.

I think life is hard for most immigrants when they come to the United States, however I have been living in the United States for almost four years now and I live a luxurious life. One day I got in an accident, but I survived. Now I'm feeling very well, thanks to God.

When I Came to the United States
Abshiro Rage, Minneapolis

My name is Abshiro Rage. I was born in Somalia, but I grew up in Kenya—mostly in the Dadaab refugee camps. I completed eighth grade in Kenya before making my way to the United States of America. I flew from Nairobi to London to New York to Boston. I was with five members of my family.

When I came to Boston, my first surprise was bedbugs. I thought America was a wonderful country that was already civilized and they wouldn't have bedbugs. When I came to my apartment, I slept the night and in the morning, I saw my arms were red and itchy. I wondered what happened, because I didn't have any idea about the problem. After a while, I went to the hospital, and they told me that it wasn't a big problem; it was just bedbugs. I said, "What? But I'm not in Africa. I'm in America!" They laughed at me and they said, "We first saw this problem just a few years ago, but it isn't a big problem." And really, that surprised me.

Minnesota Is a Good State
Omar Roble, Minneapolis

My country, Somalia, has problems that started in 1991. I was a businessman in Mogadishu. I sold sugar, oil, spaghetti and other things families need. I worked from 5:00 a.m. to 9:00 p.m. In 1991, my children and I ran! We could take nothing with us.

Now my children and I have a house in Minnesota. We came to Minneapolis in December 2001. I don't like any other city. I understand it here. Minnesota is a very good state. It helps people. I am going to school at Volunteers of America Adult High School. I have health care and I am safe.

This is a good state for us.

Omar Roble is originally from Somalia.

My Life
Ayawavi Akpaglo, Rosemount

I am from Togo, West Africa, a little country between Ghana and Benin. I started elementary school when I was seven years old. I got my certificate in 1970. I went to high school in 1971 and I got my high school diploma in 1975. That year, I also had my first son. I was married and soon was the mother of four children. In 1978, I had a teaching job at the local elementary school. I taught for 30 years. I became a widow in 2005 and my son sponsored me to come to the US to take care of my grandchildren. My first impression of the US was seeing a lot of snow, which I never saw before in my life. Now my goal is to learn English and find a part-time job.

The Four Seasons in America
Mai Lia Xiong, Minneapolis

I like the four seasons in America. They are very different from each other. The four seasons are winter, spring, summer and fall.

In the wintertime every leaf falls off the trees. Snow falls from the sky, and it's very cold, wet and white.

In the springtime, there's lots of rainfall, and grass and trees start to grow and have leaves again. In the summertime, it gets very hot and sticky. I like to go walking in the park and have picnics during the summer season.

In the fall season, I like the colors of all the trees. Some leaves turn red, orange and yellow. And then they fall off the trees to the ground. It makes everything very beautiful and yet very miserable too.

My favorite season is springtime, because I like it when the flowers start to bloom and new life begins. Birds come back to have babies and insects, too. So what season do you like the most?

Winter
Iryna Rabushka, Coon Rapids

Winter!
snowy and beautiful
drink hot chocolate
celebrate holidays, go sledding, snow pants, snowshoes, sandals, shorts
eat ice-cream, drink juice, play tennis
sunny and warm
Summer!

Iryna Rabushka is originally from Belarus.

Winter Poem
Anonymous, Saint Cloud

Winter looks like white shining snow after the winter storm.
Winter sounds like snow blowers running in the street.
Winter smells like dark chocolate in the warm kitchen.
Winter tastes like cookies with different shapes of Christmas.
Winter feels like happiness around the Christmas tree and Nativity set.

I love winter.

My Quiet Place
Lidia L. Juárez, Elk River

My quiet place is located 45 minutes away from my home in Mexico. It is the beach called "Playa Escondida." It is so beautiful and special to me. I love to walk along the beach and look around for little holes. Pretty much every time, I found a hole in the sand, automatically I knew that it was time for me to have fun playing with the crabs; I dig a hole and follow them everywhere. It's so fun to do that. There are times when they get to the water before I even have a chance to touch them. Another activity that I enjoyed a lot was riding a horse in the afternoon going along the water and seeing the sunset. At this particular beach, you can see how the sea water connects with the fresh water. It is so magical because the sea water has these big waves, but the fresh water doesn't. You have to be there to understand more about this place; I call it "My Quiet Place." Everything in there is natural and wild; no humans have put their hands there. When nighttime arrives, nothing is better than having a bonfire and enjoying the quiet of the place and looking at the sky full of stars. The moon is all that you have for light.

The sound of the waves and the birds gives you indescribable peace and relaxation and joy that takes any stress away from anyone.

It's just a magic paradise.

Coming to America
Hanifa Ghedi, Rochester

Coming to America has changed my life in many different ways. Since coming to America, I know I need to watch what I eat, I know the importance of getting education, and I know how to deal with people.

First, I learned I needed to watch what I eat. Before I came to America, I didn't care what I ate or when I ate. I was overweight. The first couple of months, I didn't change my habit of eating. One day as I was watching TV, I saw people who were struggling with their weight and couldn't control what they ate. Afterwards, I knew I had to change my way of eating or else, as the guy on the TV said, I would die from heart failure. Since then, I have learned to eat healthy food and control my hunger.

Second, getting an education has never been that important to me. I always used to think that education was not for me. But coming to America, I realized that with hard work and determination, everything is possible. I learned the value of getting education. If I want to advance in life, I have to work hard in school and get my education. Life without education is hard and worthless; education opens up a lot of opportunities.

Third, I learned how to deal with people in different ways. I used to treat people like they were not human beings. Since coming to America, I learned to adapt to people with different personalities. For example, if I want to make a friend, I need to treat them with respect. By being friendly towards people, they will treat me with respect. As my mom once told me, treat others the way you want to be treated.

The few years I have been in America, I learned to watch what I eat, learned the importance of education and dealing with people. I hope to continue to improve my life every year I am in this wonderful country.

My Village
Phong PH Nguyen, Saint Louis Park

Vy Da, my village, is not so poetic as most of your villages. That is, there is not a river winding around it nor a small boat drifting along the deep blue stream.

But Vy Da is a barn of rice which can feed

thousands of people. The land is fertile; the inhabitants are industrious and hardworking and patient. So, all over my village, there is absolutely not a piece of uncultivated land. Vy Da is not only an immense field but also a region of trees and fruit. Large gardens are full of ripe fruit of all seasons. There are also hills of high bamboos reaching into the blue sky, a symbol of strong vitality in the minds of sincere peasants.

I have been living in Minnesota now. I miss my village very much.

Phong PH Nguyen is 46 years old and is originally from Vietnam.

Indian Festival
Vani, Hopkins

Diwali is one of the biggest Hindu festivals, celebrated with great enthusiasm and happiness in India. We celebrate Diwali in October or in November during the no moon day. Diwali is one of the most important government holidays in India. On that day every store and public service will close.

Once there was an evil giant called Naragasura. He was very harmful to people. He was killing all the citizens without any reason. They complained to Lord Krishna about him. Finally Krishna killed that giant. Lord asked him his final wish. His wish was all the people should be happy on this day that he was killed and they should take an oil bath and wear new clothes. His wish was granted by Lord Krishna. This is the history of celebrating Diwali festival.

On Diwali, most of the people won't sleep before that night. Women will decorate their hands with mehandi or hena and with nail polish. Diwali is the best period for making a lot of money for the small business vendors. They will open their stores for 24 hours. They will give lots of good offers to the people. We can get most things in a buy-one-get-one-free offer.

During this festival, we wake up early in the morning and take an oil bath. We will make a variety of foods, especially sweets and snacks, and will make lot of cultural foods to share with our friends and neighbors. If one of the family members is working away from their home town, they will go back to home for these celebrations. Even if they are in foreign countries, people will plan to go back home for this. We will have lunch with our family members together. Children will have a lot of fun with the fire crackers. Younger ones will receive blessings and money from the elder ones. Most of the people will go to the temple and do special pooja.

In the evening after 6 o' clock, we will decorate the house full of lights. So Diwali is also known as a "Light Festival." Diwali diyas (candles) are one of the major attractions. Multicolored diyas look fabulous. Nowadays Diwali festivals are celebrated around the world.

> I like and love nature everywhere. But I think, in my city, nature is very lovely because of the weather. It has a very nice smell.

Fall
Sima Noroozi, Coon Rapids

My favorite Fall seasons are both in the USA and in my city. I think Fall in the many states in the USA is very nice and beautiful because of the many great and different trees and different colors in this country. I like and love nature everywhere. But I think, in my city, nature is very lovely because of the weather. It has a very nice smell. This weather I remember when I was in my country. In this season, I usually walked outside every day. Sometimes I walked with my mother or my family and sometimes I walked with my friends too. But here I am almost alone, and I haven't a partner for going walking or sharing my emotions with. I hope to find my new favorite friends.

Sima Noroozi is 46 years old and is originally from Tehran, Iran.

Untitled
FB, Saint Louis Park

My name is Faduma. I came from Somalia. I was born and grew up in the capital city, Mogadishu. Mogadishu is a coastal and cosmopolitan city. At that time, Mogadishu was where Somalis, Arabs, Indians, and Italians lived together side by side peacefully. Mogadishu has bazaar markets even today. I cannot forget the nice smells and colors. I remember those days. I used to go shopping with my family. They were the best days of my life. When I was in my country, I graduated from high school and my dream was journalism, but it did not happen because by that time, the civil war had started. During that war, I did not only lose my dream, I even lost my beloved father. After that time, the rest of my family and I moved to Kenya. I married and had five kids. After that, we got the opportunity to come to Minnesota. Today, Minnesota has given me back my old dream, because we have unlimited opportunities here.

America
Isir Egeh, Minneapolis

On my first trip to America, I was afraid because it was a strange country. I thought I would see a different Earth. I thought I would see different people and different land. I had heard that night and day were different than what our country had. I thought American cities all had tall buildings, but I first came to Charlotte, North Carolina, and it had a lot of small houses similar to our country houses. When I was in Nairobi, Kenya, at the airport, I first took escalators and I was scared. I thought everywhere in America there would be escalators. I still don't like escalators. However, what I thought and what I was met with were different. I saw a nice country and met nice and helpful people in America. Two things that were a little bit harder for me to get used to were the time and the weather, but now I have gotten used to them.

Untitled
Hassan Omar, Minneapolis

The Twin Cities is indeed my favorite place to live. The reason is simple. I left my country, Somalia, in 1991 after the Civil War started. I thought that no matter where I went in the world, I would never feel peaceful and secure again. For a while, I was right.

My family and I fled Somalia and crossed the border into Kenya. The Kenyan police beat us and harmed us badly. They did not want us to come into their country, but we did not have a choice. Finally, the Kenyan government put us in a refugee camp about 80 km east of Somalia. The situation there was terrible. For example, there was never enough food, the water was dirty, and armed men were looting and sometimes raping women in front of the Kenyan authorities.

I left Kenya in 1998 and moved to the US. I felt I was safe again in Minneapolis, Minnesota. I found a job and a place to live. I also found peace and respect, but that is not all.

The Twin Cities has the largest Somali community in North America. Here, I do not feel homesick or alone. Not only that, but I can find all kinds of stuff that I used to enjoy when I was in Somalia, such as Somali food, clothes, books and entertainment. Here in the Twin Cities, I feel safe and I have a lot of opportunities. Somalia is no longer peaceful and stable so I cannot go back, but the Twin Cities is my favorite place and my second home.

From a Refugee Camp to Freedom
Bhagirath Dhungana, Saint Paul

I was born in Bhutan and lived there until 1961. I spent more than seventeen years in a refugee camp in Nepal. In the refugee camp, I worked as a volunteer in Community Health Service. There are seven refugee camps in Nepal. I was from Timai Camp, in the eastern part of Nepal.

After seventeen years, the International Organization of Immigration wanted to resettle Bhutanese refugees in one of seven countries. I chose the United States to start my new life. I arrived in the US on August 5th, 2008. I am happy to start my new life in the US, because we have equal rights here. I never got a chance to study in the refugee camp, but in the United States, I get the opportunity to study. I am proud to be a US resident. I feel safe and equal in the US. In the refugee camp in Nepal, I did not feel safe, nor did I feel equal.

Bhagirath Dhungana is originally from Bhutan.

The Winter
Silvia Martínez, Minneapolis

In my country, the weather is not cold like Minnesota. In Minnesota, the weather is too cold and is very dangerous, people fall on the snow and they break their bones. I fell on the snow and I broke my hand, and I can't work for many weeks. The snow is dangerous too for drivers because the drivers can't drive. Many cars crash on the freeway. The snow is so beautiful; I like it so much, but sometimes it is not good for my body.

Silvia Martínez is originally from Mexico.

Timeline of My Life
Fatuma Abdullahi, Burnsville

I was born in Somalia in 1988. I have four sisters and two brothers. My father died. My family continued to live in Somalia until 1999.

Daniel Weston, Duluth

Then we moved to Kenya. I lived there from age four to twenty years old. I started school in Kenya. Then I moved to the United States in 2007. I worked at an electronic processing place in San Jose, California until December 2008. I moved to Minnesota at the end of December 2008. I go to school in the Hubbs Center now.

Hand Warmer
Luta Tshihamba, Saint Louis Park

Wisconsin has seen enough of me. What next? I used to live in California after I left the Congo in 1997. Barbara and Bill, my son's in-laws, invited my husband Remy and me to celebrate Christmas with them in Wisconsin. It was the first time going with my son Paul and his family, including his sister-in-law's family. I was looking forward to seeing them again and beind together with the whole family. I was thinking about that unique celebration to thank God for taking care of me in the Congo.

Bill and Barbara were very happy about having the house full of us and they prepared lots of goodies too. Bill arranged sightseeing and a sleigh ride. Before we left for the trip, Andrea had warned them that I was not accustomed to being in cold weather. Barbara was worried about me and she gave me some warm clothes to prevent me from getting cold. In addition, she gave me a hand warmer in case I needed it. She believed that I wasn't going to complain about being cold. I felt warm enough and like a good-looking woman in a fancy coat, hood, gloves, and boots. I felt powerful when I started walking towards the car, believing that I was capable of challenging the cold weather.

We had a nice sightseeing trip and then we went to the last place for the sleigh ride. I was excited about being carried in the sleigh behind the horse. When I got out of the car, it was 30 degrees below zero with wind chill. All 18 of us sat in different sleighs and we started riding. I was very cold and my nose started running. I held the warmer in my hands to warm me up. The wind continued to blow so hard on my uncovered face that I wasn't participating in the conversation anymore. I took advantage of using the warmer to cover my nose instead of warming my hands.

Barbara felt bad about making me uncomfortable because it seemed strange to use the warmer like that. When we came back, everybody was shocked. They started joking, laughing and having fun about it. Before I knew it, Barbara was taking my picture for an important souvenir. We still talk about the story of the hand warmer to this day.

Luta Tshihamba is originally from Congo.

Happy in Minneapolis
Hajia Abdi, Minneapolis

I was living in Mogadishu, Somalia before the Civil War. Then I went to Nairobi, Kenya. Then I got a sponsor, so I could come to the United States of America. I live in Minneapolis, Minnesota. I have lived here for around five years. I am very happy in Minneapolis, because I study English, math, science and computers. I am very happy about that.

My Favorite Season
Emily Balderas, Elk River

I am not a fan of summer. Where most people see bugs, a break from school, and a tan by the pool, I see mosquitoes, humidity and road construction. Mosquitoes seem to find me, with or without a thick layer of bug spray. I feel like I must be wearing a big sign that says "Bite Me" on it. It's bad enough to feel dehydrated and overheated by the damaging rays of the sun, but I enjoy this while pitted with itchy bumps all over my body.

Have I mentioned the road construction? Minnesota always has road construction going on regardless of the season, but from May through September it multiplies like a fourth grader. There is no better misuse of my time than being stuck in traffic in a hot car due to the transportation department's poor planning. To me, summer means bug bites, bad weather and driving irritation. No thank you!

Life in Minnesota
Johnathan Saw, Saint Paul

I arrived in Minnesota on May 22nd, 2004. My sister, who lived in the US for about ten years, picked me up from the airport to go to her home. Everything that I saw along the road made me surprised. Most of all, the buildings in Minnesota looked strong, neat, and tidy. Many different races lived in this city. Maybe the African-American people were the largest amount in this city. Wherever you went, you could meet the African-American people—at least one or two people walking on the sidewalk. All people use vehicles and can go anywhere. I like Minnesota and need to enjoy it all the time.

Johnathan Saw is originally from Burma.

My First Day in the USA
Angel Herrera, Shakopee

On my first day in America, I was scared and excited. Scared because of the way I came to America. I had to pay someone to take me across the border from Tijuana, Mexico to San Diego, California, hidden in the back seat of a classic car. But, I was excited to know a new country, different culture, people, language, and food.

I remember my first meal in America was Chinese food. I had never tried it before, but I like it now. I remember being happy to see my cousin. He took me on a tour around the town. What I remembered most is all the different looking houses and tall buildings. I stayed in California about two months before I moved to Minnesota.

When I got to Minnesota, I think that was the day when I felt in America. California was a little bit like Mexico City.

The first thing I saw when I left the airport was the snow. It was my first time seeing the snow. I was really impressed to see all the houses covered with snow and people plowing the snow and putting salt on the roads using dump trucks.

My cousin took me to a big mall, and I saw many people shopping and having fun. That was my first time listening to all the people speaking English. After dinner and walking around the stores, we went to downtown Minneapolis and on our way there I remember seeing many houses with real snowmen on their front yards.

That was the day when I started my new life in United States of America.

Angel Herrera is 30 years old and is originally from Mexico City.

My Hometown in Ecuador
Anonymous, Minneapolis

I lived in a village in Ecuador called Azugues where most of the people are farmers. Their crops are corn, potatoes and wheat. Some have cattle, and some of them are construction workers. There are three kinds of religions in my village: Catholic, Lutheran and Baptist. All of them have churches. There is no racism or discrimination between each other. They are respectful. All three religions are community organizations. They work together. The community works hard against illegal things, such as drugs and thieving. In earlier years, the leader of the community was a man who had not finished high school. Since 2000, a man who finished college became high leader of the community. The leader works with different organizations, including the government. What's most important is that their village is building more schools and doing other things too. Before 2005, the village school didn't have a computer lab. They had one language class in Spanish, but now they are learning one more language in English.

I Am Lucky
Fadumo Aden, Minneapolis

I am lucky because I do many things for my family and myself. I am lucky because I came to America. Because coming to America helps me to do a lot of things. I am really lucky because when I came to America I didn't get any problems and the first company I applied to hired me. I am lucky because I support my family and send money. I am lucky because I am an ESL student and I have excellent teachers who always help us to learn nice ways.

Fadumo Aden is originally from Somalia.

Coming to America
Shukri Naghiye, Rochester

Coming to America was so different from home. It was different than where I used to live because of the weather, transportation, and finding jobs. Where I grew up, the weather was always warm, but that all changed when I came to America. The first time I came to America, it was summer, and that was the first time I saw a tornado. After a while, winter started, and that was the first time I saw snow. When I saw all that snow, I was scared that we may get stuck at home or at work. I used to hear stories about the snow and how dangerous it can get. After awhile, I got used to America's weather and even learned how to drive in the snow.

It is very important to have your own transportation when you live in America. It was hard for me to find a job because of lack of transportation, and the biggest obstacle that

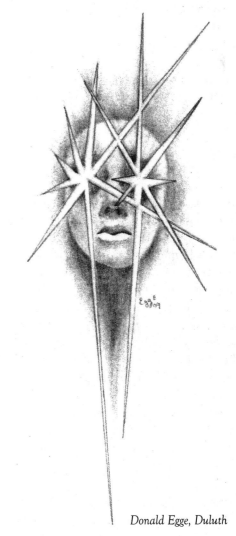

Donald Egge, Duluth

Visions of Home - 31

I had to deal with was learning how to drive. Back home, women usually don't worry about driving, because men think it is their job to operate big machines. With my friend's help, I had my driver's license in nine months.

Finding a job was harder that I had thought. I could barely speak English, and that made it difficult for me to find any job. When I came to America, I was thinking I would be able to find a good job, but after four months, I did not get anything. Because I wasn't able to communicate well, I wasn't able to find a job. I had to realize that I need to improve my communication by attending some English classes in order to achieve anything.

In conclusion, America is a great country because it gives a good opportunity for many immigrant people. I am one of those people who found a new home and hopeful future in America.

My Life
Lirouwane Sow, Saint Michael

I grew up in Guinea in West Africa, and my parents had four children: my big brother, my sister, me and a younger sister. I came to America 16 months ago to live with my wonderful sister (who has done everything for me), her lovely husband and their three beautiful children. I am thankful to my father, a doctor, because he wanted a better education for us. I'm also thankful to my mother who taught chemistry, because she always taught us how to respect, love and forgive the people around us. I remember when she took our food and gave it to people who really needed it. I was mad, but now I understand why she did that. She passed away in 2005. I know she's proud of us where she is right now.

I'm happy to be in the US now, but I still miss many things about my country. In Guinea, children can play outside safely, and their parents don't have to worry about them. I miss holiday celebrations in my country too. I remember when Id-al-Fitr arrived and everyone was excited, with new clothes and shoes. We ate a lot of food, and children got money and candy. I miss my young sister, who's married and in New York, and I miss my brother and father in Guinea.

Even though there is much I miss about my homeland, I am happy about my present life. My vision is to study at a medical school, but first I have to learn English. I came to the Saint Michael Community Education center, where I met wonderful teachers who don't care about the color of your skin or how you look. They're always there to help us study and understand English and American culture. They do whatever they can to teach us, and I appreciate them a lot. In my class, I feel like I'm in a family with everybody caring for each other. The students from different countries are interesting and kind. I also like Minnesota very much, except for the cold winter.

In conclusion, my life has its joys and sorrows, but I am happy about my past, present and future.

My Life in the USA
Tshibola Gemaine, Prior Lake

Every day, I wake up at 5:30 a.m. to wake up my daughter, because she must walk to take the bus for Normandale College at 6:20 a.m. After that, I must check the other children so they don't miss the bus, and I help my young child to take a shower and to prepare him for school, because he is still in elementary school. I'm the last one to leave home for my English class.

After my English class, I come back before everybody. I cook the food, and I wait for them to come to eat. After we eat, we rest and begin the homework. I help my children to do their homework. If we finish the homework, we clean dishes, put each thing in place and we watch TV. At 10:00 p.m., we pray and go to bed.

Every Saturday and Sunday, I don't work. My children clean the house and clothes and cook food. I'm at rest.

Looking Back
Marie Edoh Gnronfoun, Minneapolis

I have left my beautiful country—warm, tropical Togo. It has the beautiful ocean, and the rich soil in which grow many different fruits, vegetables, and grains. I want to just smell home again, but it is too far away. I have missed all the natural foods and the fresh fish, shrimp, and crabs.

I think about my relatives, friends, and co-workers. I yearn for our big house to be right here in the United States of America. We had a big compound, fruit trees, and many different flowers and trees on our property.

We make a little tent in the front of the house in which we have many different kinds of items like sugar, peanuts, bananas, oranges, lemons, cold water, candies, bread, cookies and many, many more for people who pass by, so they can buy for their needs.

My Scary Experience
A.G., Saint Cloud

One day, I was in my father's house, and we were talking about ghosts. Suddenly, we heard a little girl crying, and we thought that it was the wind. But when we went outside, it wasn't windy. Then I turned on the radio and they were talking about ghosts. It was the middle of the night when we were listening to the radio, and suddenly we heard the little girl crying again, but this time it was louder and we got scared.

I asked my father, "What's going on, Dad?" and he said, "Don't worry, it is OK." So he turned the radio off and we went to sleep. While we were sleeping, it felt like someone was pulling my foot. I screamed loudly, and my dad came quickly to my bedroom and asked me what happened. I told him that it felt like someone was pulling my foot and when I screamed, I saw the little girl pass by my door and move toward the kitchen. My father said, "Let's go to the kitchen and you will see that no one is there." When we arrived there it was a mess! Dishes, food, and pots that had been on the shelves were now on the floor. My dad screamed, and I said, "Can you see that I was telling you the truth and you didn't believe me?" Then he said, "But now I believe you."

Since that time we don't turn on the radio because we are very scared. Instead, we watched TV.

A.G. is originally from Mexico.

Who Am I?
Truc Mai Tran Thi, Andover

My name is Truc Mai. I am a young Brazilian woman. I guess I'm a woman without clarity of identification—Vietnamese, Brazilian or Paraguayan. That is sometimes complicated to explain. My blood is Vietnamese, my culture is Brazilian, and my nationality is Paraguayan. What kind of woman am I?

I'm polyglot, calm, affectionate, friendly, and fun. I have a bit of each country, but everyone who doesn't know me thinks I'm Thai or Hawaiian.

I have had the great privilege to learn other languages because my parents are of Vietnamese descent, I was born in Paraguay, and I ended up in Brazil. I concluded my studies with a degree in Business Administration with emphasis on quality control.

I love traveling and meeting new cultures of other countries, but there is nothing better than my country—my small town of Foz do Iguaçu, where I grew up with my friends and lived around nature.

My life is always open to something new—learning new stuff and meeting new friends.

A Travel Memory
Anonymous, Saint Cloud

One day I was traveling in the USA; I came from Ethiopia and my little daughter who was with me was scared of white people, and most everybody in America is white. At the time, I was at the Washington airport. A lot of police suspected I was a terrorist and took me to a special place to do a body search. A lot of people were watching me, and my little daughter was screaming harder and harder. That is something unforgettable to me!

Ramadan
Deqo Yasin, Minneapolis

My name is Deqo Yasin and I am from Somalia. Ramadan is the ninth month of the Islamic lunar calendar. Muslims observe the Ramadan fast, one of the five pillars of Islam, for 29 or 30 days. Fasting means completely abstaining from food, drink, smoking and sexual relations from sunrise to sunset.

The Islamic lunar year is shorter than the Gregorian calendar by eleven days. Fasting rotates through the year, so Muslims experience it in different seasons. Ramadan reminds Muslims to be kind and generous to the poor. It also teaches patience and self control. Muslims eat a predawn meal called Suhur to help them with the fasting. Then they break the fast with a special meal after sunset, beginning with dates, sambusa, porridge, and water, juice or tea. Some families eat dinner right away. Others relax and serve dinner later. There are usually more pastas, sweets and delicacies. After that, it is family time when all family members come together. Children cherish the delicious food prepared especially for Ramadan. They are not required to fast until the age of puberty. However, children at the elementary level start fasting early to get used to it and it is quite common for children as young as 9 years old to fast.

Usually, Muslims use a local sighting of the moon or personal observation or consultation with others to determine the end of the month. Other times, if the moon cannot be seen locally, a confirmed sighting anywhere in the world is used to determine the end of the month. Muslims would like schools and employers to be flexible in accommodating the short notice of Eid al Fitr, observed at the end of Ramadan.

> My life is always open to something new–learning new stuff and meeting new friends

My Little Country
E.L., Saint Paul

I was born in a tiny little country called Estonia, what is nowadays a part of the European Union. My home country is really small, because the population is slightly over one million. But anyway, it absolutely doesn't matter how huge or small the county is. The main thing for me is that it is the most wonderful, beautiful and lovely place in the whole world; it holds a lot of history, nostalgic memories of my childhood, and of course, the amazing Gulf of Finland.

Estonia has two large islands called Saaremaa and Hiiumaa. Hiiumaa is a bit smaller. Furthermore, there are also a few smaller islands. The biggest city and the capital city is Tallinn, where I lived until I moved to the US. Estonia borders two countries—the Russian Federation on the east side and Latvia on the south—so these two are the closest neighbors of my country.

Estonia has lots of charming places. My favorite one is the oldest part of the city called Tallinn. If you get there one day, you will understand what I am talking about. You will find narrow, picturesque streets paved with rocks, which you will not see in contemporary towns. Tiny little stores and pubs are everywhere. And the most famous and distinctive features of Old Town are the red roofs all over.

Therefore, if you do like temperate climates and do not mind a bit of rain or if travel is your passion and you have never been in the northeastern part of the European Union, come visit Estonia—maybe you will love it as much as I do.

I Was Scared
Lukman Abdile, Saint Cloud

Sometime back in the last year, I think it was November 1st because it was Halloween, and it was early in the morning, like 5:30 a.m., I had just finished my work and I wanted to leave from my workplace to go home. As I opened the door, someone who covered all his body with grasses or something like dry leaves said to me, "Happy Halloween!" I said, "What!" and I was really scared.

Lukman Abdile is originally from Somalia.

My Story
Lorenzo Torregrossa, Oakdale

My name is Lorenzo Torregrossa. I was born in Licata, a beautiful town in Sicily, Italy.

I had a fantastic childhood until the age of twelve when I lost my father. Months later, I moved to the north of Italy in Biella, a town in the Alps, where I went to work to support my mom and three little sisters.

I started work in construction because my dad was a builder, and I wanted to do the same job. At the age of twenty, I had my own construction company. Since 1992, I would come to Minnesota to visit my cousin in Minneapolis where he had an Italian restaurant. It was on one of these visits that I met my wife, who is a sales representative.

I moved to Minnesota in September 2001. We got married in December 2001. When I moved to Minnesota, I did not speak or write any English. I started to work for a nice construction company until I learned a little English. Then, I started my own company. I decided to go to ESL to improve my English, because I need it for my business. Meanwhile, I became a US citizen, and I am proud of it and to be part of this beautiful country.

Ethiopian Independence
Weynshet Tesfaye, Apple Valley

I come from Ethiopia. Most European countries tried to stretch their empire over Ethiopia. Italy tried to stretch its empire over Ethiopia. This started a war between Ethiopia and Italy. Ethiopian people believe in God and believe they shouldn't have weapons. The place of the war is called the "Battle of Adwa." Every year on February 23rd, Ethiopia celebrates its independence from Italy.

The Different Lifestyle
Antonieta Sánchez, Owatonna

When I moved to the United States, it was very hard for me because it has different traditions and language. However, it was very interesting to know about other countries and their cultures.

When I lived in Mexico, I really couldn't understand why people moved to the United States looking for the American Dream. However, now that I have had the opportunity to stay here, I can see that the lifestyle is very different. People here live with more technology which makes things easier and more comfortable for the people.

In Mexico, life is so hard. People have to work very hard all day and the salaries are very poor, so that you cannot have many of the things that you have in the United States.

I am glad to stay in the United States because I am looking for new opportunities. I am learning the language, the culture and I love this country because each day, I can learn new interesting things different from my country.

My Dream
Hawa Roba, Golden Valley

I have a dream that one day I will be a nursing assistant and help the community to help other people in need.

I have a dream that one day this country will have the economy back, so the American people will have good jobs. Then everybody will have the dream back.

History of the Oromo People
Mary Kitila, Woodbury

The Oromo are one of the Cushitic-speaking groups of people. The Oromo have variations in skin color and physical characteristics, ranging from Hamitic to Nilotic. A brief look at the early history of some of the peoples who occupied Northeastern Africa sheds some light on the ethnic origin of the Oromo.

Cushitic speakers have inhabited Northeastern and Eastern Africa for as long as recorded history exists. Oromo have several clans. The Oromo are said to be of two major groups or moieties descended from the two houses, wives, of the Person Oromo represented by Borana and Barentu. (Barenttuma) Borana was the senior (Anyafa), and Barentu was the junior (Quitisu). Such a dichotomy is quite common in Oromo society and serves some aspect of their political and social life.

The Oromo make up 50 percent of the population of the Ethiopian Empire. They are found in all the regions of the Ethiopian Empire except for Gondar. They make up a large proportion of the population of Llubbador, Arsi Baule, Shawa, Hurage, Wallo, Wallagga, Sidamo, and Kafa. They are also found in neighboring countries such as Kenya and Somalia. Out of the 50 nations of Africa, only four have an ethnic population that is larger than the Oromo people.

Mary Kitila is originally from Oromia, Ethiopia.

Real or Non-Real
María Bustillos, Clearwater

When I was a child, my uncle told me about a white horse you can see on dark nights and that he touched the tail and the horse disappeared. I don't know if it's true, but he scared me. Some people told the story, and when I went out of the house, I remembered that and was scared again.

María Bustillos is originally from Chihuahua, Mexico.

Remembering
Laura Flores, Minneapolis

I love to remember the beautiful nights of my Mexico.
I love to remember the birth of my children.
I love to remember my childhood.
I love remembering every day of my life!
I love remembering because remembering is living!

Laura Flores is originally from Mexico.

I Have a Dream
Hassan Budeye, Minneapolis

I have a dream that one day I will be happy about that dream after I see it.
My dad told me, "You will be a teacher or a good student."
I have a dream someday my family will have a party for the marriage of my sister.
I like it.
I have a dream that one day my country will have a nice government because right now we don't have a good government.
I like it.
I have a dream that one day all people in the world will be nice—everybody to everybody else.

Lady Liberty
Chad Erickson, Duluth

Natural and pure, like a river's mighty flow,
Beautiful and distinct, like wind-driven snow,
My oh my, her enchanting glow,
More inspiring than moon-lit snowy lakes.
Strong and true, like a friendship over time,
Magical and unique, for each day we seek,
With the power of each passing week,
More meaningful than our future we foresee.
Strong and tall, she stands above them all,
Smart and righteous, despite what divides us.
More soothing than gifted ancestors' traits,
Soft and delicate, like the things we don't forget.
Sunrises and sunsets, like our beloved pets.
Destiny is how we meet them
More fulfilling than the air we breathe
Life and liberty, like our civilized society
Riches and poverty, we're molded like pottery.
The economy is how we survive,
More emotional than a first love.

Wilma Griebel, Southern Minnesota

Visions of Home - 37

Dreaming
John Thurston, Annandale

I sat on the shore of a stream the other day and dreamt of how the West was won. I listened to the water laughing in the bright sun.

I wondered how it would feel to ride upon a snow-crested ridge and look out across forty miles known only to antelope, Indians and buffalo; to stand on a snowy peak and wonder how far the plains might go.

How it must have felt to explore the western lands with the wind blowing the fresh smell of the pines and that of cedar and pine burning to make your coffee. What was it like to witness the vast expanse of the grass sea and the wind blowing the clouds across the desert's face?

I wonder about the fears, broiling venison over the fire and not knowing whether or not you would rise again, with the chill of the crisp morning air filling your lungs, or the song of a mountain spring filling your ears.

I can only imagine riding across the desert, watching a storm build upon the mountains; the tumbleweeds trying to outrun the wind with no boundaries or fences. How grand it must have been watching an antelope perk up at the anger of the sound of far off thunder, now alert with all its senses.

As I lay there watching the sun dance upon the water like the stars in a beautiful woman's eyes when she is gleaming, I realize these days are all but gone, but nothing can stop me from dreaming.

My Homeland
Nhia Doua Yang, Saint Paul

Laos is the name of my homeland.
It is a beautiful place with green hills.
The breeze brushes against my face,
Making me carefree.

Laos is the name of my homeland.
There are many happy faces everywhere.
It has many beautiful cultures.

Laos is the name of my homeland.
It is the place I want to visit.

In Laos I walk under the flowing bright stars
and the shiny moonlight that leads my way.

Wishing
Damon Dickerson, Virginia

Wishing to be with my family
Wishing my shame and guilt
Would be set free
Wishing love would overcome
My jealousy
Wishing my life was different
As I'm always feeling alone.

Artist
Jaime R. Dejesus, Duluth

I like to draw and watch football.
I also like to sing, but above all
drawing will be my thing.
Drawing animals like a beautiful deer
would probably be a cool career.
So who's to know or who's to say
that I might be like Bob Ross some day.
So until then I'll tell you all,
that a happy tree may never fall.
So thank you, God, for this wonderful gift
that you have given me,
so that I can draw a member of a friend's family.
So I thank you for listening to my poem,
because I might draw you some day;
You never know...

Jaime R. Dejesus is 38 years old and is originally from Puerto Rico.

My Country
Anonymous, Minneapolis

I miss my country.
I was born in Morocco.
I was living in Casablanca.
I had a good life when I was there.
I miss my mom and my dad.
I miss everything like family, food, weather, sea, people, falls, mountains...
I miss I miss I miss my land, it was like heaven.
I was traveling a lot when I was there.
I have a dream that my life would be like before.
I remember my first day when I came to the USA, it was a big dream for me.
I miss, I miss, I miss...

Take a Deep Breath
Yellow Leaf, Maplewood

Take a deep breath
When you fear
Take a deep breath
When you have a tear
Take a deep breath
When you cannot make things clear
Take a deep breath
When you miss me, Dear
Take a deep breath
When I have not yet appeared
Take a deep breath
When you are going to pull on your gear
Take a deep breath
When you are looking at your rear
Take a deep breath
When everything is clear, change your gear, and come to me, Dear
I love you.

Yellow Leaf is originally from Italy.

Freezing
Rocio Estrada, Brooklyn Park

Frozen water in winter time
Rain some days
Emergency alert, when the time is bad
Everybody needs to be careful if driving
Zero degrees a few days
In the winter, a lot of people love to skate
News about the temperature all the time
Good idea is to drink hot chocolate.

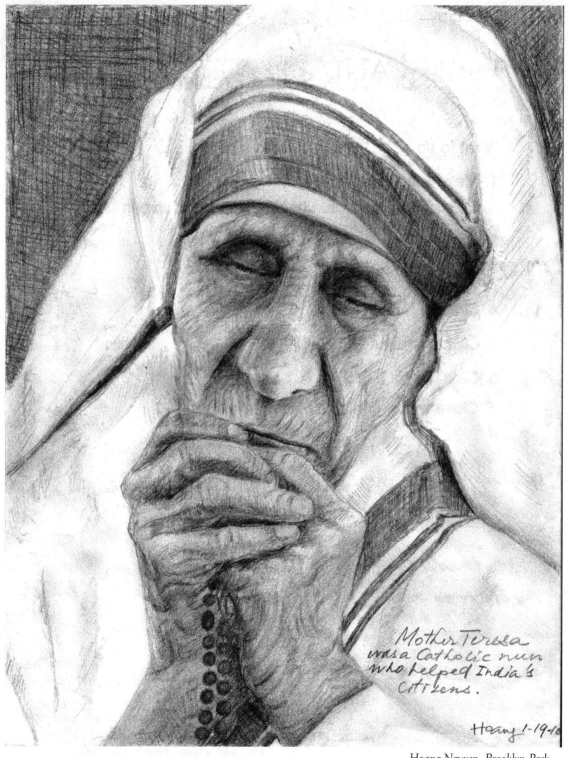

Hoang Nguyen, Brooklyn Park

Struggles and Victories

The Lady Who Tried to Help
Hoang Nguyen, Brooklyn Park

The lady I admire so much is the person who gave all of her life to serve all the slum people, where human life seems to have no value. In the beginning, she walked down the street giving food to the hungry, washed dirty bodies with illnesses, helped the handicapped, visited the families which needed help with something, cared for and nursed the old people, and spoonfed those too weak to feed themselves. She also did not forget the children, who lived without the care of their parents or related persons, and more.

She started each day in silence for several months and several years. Later, the world looked back on her work and gave her numerous awards. In my mind, the source of her good work came from her heart; she didn't think about any prizes.

Mother Teresa passed away after over 50 years of serving India's human life, and her Missionary of Charities are now found in over 100 countries with over 500 houses. About 4,000 sisters serve in homes for the poor, the dying, orphan children, mental patients, and many more, even in America.

Hard Times
Seila Has, Oakdale

Some people have a hard time in life from the war. Some people have a hard time in life because their family is poor. Some people have a hard time in life because they move from one place to a new place. I always think about my life. How can I get away from the hard life? Because everybody knows life is short they know life is very important. I started to understand about my life. I like my life. I want to do good things for my life. I want to make my life happy. I always help people. But I always try to get away from the problem. But I do not have good luck all the time. I will get good luck in the future.

Seila Has is originally from Cambodia.

A Difficult Experience
Hawo Jama, Eagan

My name is Hawo. I am from Somalia. My experiences are many. Some of them were very good; most of them were really bad. Every time I remember them, tears come to my eyes. One day my city was captured by the militia. They destroyed everything. Some people were able to run, but most of them chose to stay. I was one of them. I still remember the torture of the people. Women got raped. Five women came near where I was living. They were young. All of them had been raped. Two of them were really sick. They looked like they were going to die. I asked, "If all of those women got raped, what's up with those two?" The lady taking care of them told me one of them was pregnant. The other one was young and beautiful and she got more men than the others. The other thing I saw there was a young woman who just got married. She had a baby, nine days old. When they told her to open the door, she refused. Her mother told me that. She said, "I would rather die. First you will have to kill me. I won't open the door." She got killed. Those animals think they can get away with it, but one day I'm sure they are going to pay the price.

A True Story
Halima Omar, Minneapolis

One day, I ran from my country. I came to the edge of Kenya. That place is called Mahreed. It has a long river. If you wanted to go to town, you rode the boat. The boat was driven by two men. They drove the boat with a stick. When the boat stopped, it stood at the corner. Then the boat was upside down. All the people were in the water. I didn't know how to swim. My husband was waiting for me. When he saw me he ran quickly. He came in the river. He found me. He caught me in the water. We went to our home. My husband is good, and he loves me. I love him too.

Halima Omar is originally from Somalia.

Wintertime
Anonymous, Saint Paul

This was my first experience in Minnesota. I didn't have snow pants, snow boots, or a warm jacket. I didn't know how cold it was. My cousin asked me to go out with him and hunt for squirrels during the wintertime. I said, "O.K., if you want me to be your partner." Then the weekend came up, and I got ready to go out with him without snow pants, gloves, or jacket. I just wore fall clothing. When we got to the hunting area and went into the woods, there was six inches of snow. I didn't know how cold it was, because it was my first winter in Minnesota. When I stayed in the woods for five minutes, my feet, hands, ears, and nose were getting colder and colder. I didn't know what to do. My cousin was gone far away from me. I didn't know where he went, because we each went a different direction when we went into the woods.

Then I came back to the car, I didn't have any keys. The car belonged to my cousin. I stayed around the car more than three hours. Finally he came back. He asked, "Did you have any luck?" I said, "No. It was too cold." I felt frostbite all over my body. Then I said, "Could you open your car? I want to take a rest and warm up."

Then he opened the car, and I went into the car. He went back in the woods again. I started the engine and turned on the heat for awhile to warm up. Then I turned off the engine and fell asleep.

When he came back, he woke me up and we came home.

Ever since that happened to me, I have never gone out in the woods in wintertime again.

> I didn't know how cold it was, because it was my first winter in Minnesota. When I stayed in the woods for five minutes, my feet, hands, ears, and nose were getting colder and colder.

An Outsider in the U.S.
Neng Vang, Minneapolis

My wife married me in 1981. At that time, we lived in a refugee camp. After a year, in 1982, we went to Phanat Nit Khom camp to study English for six months and to get ready to come to the US. But she was pregnant again. So we had to wait until the baby was born. In 1984, we came to the US. So we went to the airport. That night, we landed in Hong Kong and stayed in a tall hotel! Many families did not know how to speak English. Four families from Cambodia came to ask me to help them. They were so scared because they didn't understand what to do or where to go or eat. Everyone was asking me for help. That night, they came to knock on my door and they all came to sleep in my room because I knew only a few words of Cambodian and little English. Most people know how to speak Thai and English. In the morning, they came to knock on my door. All of us went out to eat and got ready to come to the US.

After we landed in Los Angeles, we split up. Two families were crying because nobody could translate for them. I told them, "Don't cry. Someone will take care of you until you see your people or your relatives. Good luck."

After we landed in Minnesota, nobody picked us up. One Lao guy saw me. He came to talk to me. I gave him a phone number. I stayed there all day long until my sponsors picked me up to take me to my mother-in-law's home. They had locked the door and made me stay outside. So my brother-in-law came back from school. He asked me, "Are you my brother in-law?" I said yes, and he said, "It is too cold. Why do you stay outside?" I said that they locked the door. Then he knocked on the door. They didn't open it. Then he kicked the door and it almost broke. Then they opened the door and we both went inside. Then my mother-in-law told my wife to divorce me. But my wife said, "Mom, he didn't want to marry me. I wanted to marry him."

She did end up divorcing me later. So I think I have bad luck in my life because of my mother-in-law.

My Life with Gang Members
Anonymous, Saint Cloud

When I was little, my parents did not have much money, so we had to live in bad neighborhoods. Gang members always surrounded me because kids we grew up with got into gangs. We knew lots of them, but we were not able to hang around with them because my parents never let us. If we did, my dad would hit us with a belt.

One bad experience I had was when I was coming back from school. Two gangsters came at me and stole my money and a ring I had on me. I saw so many kids get killed around me. I swore to my mother that I was going to move out of Los Angeles so my son would not see or go through the same things that I did.

Another experience was when one of the gang members told me that my son was going to be in their gang when he grew up. That's when I said "No! I've got to get out of here."

That is how I moved to Minnesota. I like this state and the city that I live in. I live in Saint Cloud. Where I live is a good neighborhood. I feel safe with my kids.

Today I am going to school and I am about to earn my diploma.

Scary Memory
Amin, Minneapolis

When I was 10 to 16 years old, I was scared a lot. I remember I fought with my friends. I remember sometimes we fought with groups. Sometimes they hurt us

Struggles and Victories - 43

and sometimes we hurt them. I remember we played together in school, but when we went outside school, we started to fight with each other. I remember one day, someone hurt me and he ran to the home. Some of my group went to report it to the police. When the police came to me, I felt good. The police told us not to fight with each other. Then we said OK. But the next day, we saw our enemy and hit him by groups. I do remember this scary memory.

My Tragic Loss
Arcelia Reyes, Elk River

I lost my mom at 12:36 p.m. on Monday, June 26, 2006, a day embedded in my mind and heart at age 36.

I have not been able to forget the look in her eyes when she passed away or how cold she felt. I remember how she looked at me with fear, not for herself, but for my brothers and their kids. I made her a promise to always take care of my brothers; to keep our family together. She fought for her life until I spoke those words. I knew she wasn't worried about me because she knew I was a strong person. I had to organize my mom's funeral and put my pain and mourning aside. I had to be strong for my brothers and my niece and nephews. I had to explain to them that their grandma was in a better place with God.

Unfortunately, I was angry with God. I couldn't understand why He took her from me, why He didn't take me instead. Didn't he know how much my brothers needed her? Why did He do this to me? How could He take my best friend from me? What did I do to deserve this? I felt like dying. Without my mom there was no reason to live. I went on a drinking binge and started doing cocaine again. I was in a self-destruct mode and didn't care if I lived or died.

My eyes were opened by my little niece and nephew when they asked me, "Are you going to leave us too, Auntie? Please don't leave us like Mommy Carmen." I stopped and looked in the mirror and I looked like hell. I hugged my niece and nephew and told them, no, that I'd never drink around them again.

> My new life in the Thailand camp was very hard. Sometimes I sewed clothes and sometimes planted a farm.

I have made a lot of mistakes in my life that I regret. My pride and joy are my kids and my brothers. I have helped them through this tragedy of losing my mother, best friend and hero.

Even though I'm 38 years old now, I still need her more than ever. I'd give anything for one more day with her. I know in my heart she is in a better place. But I can't help like feeling that God took her away from me too soon. I'm still not ready to let her go. Maybe one day I'll be able to understand, but for now, I just can't do it. I know I'm being selfish, but I want my mom back. My conscience is at ease, because I was with her 'til the bitter end. But it hurts just the same.

So I ask, please don't take your mother for granted, because you don't know what you have 'til it's gone.

New Life in the Refugee Camp and America
Bounhom Sayachack, Minneapolis

I was a soldier in Laos, and then later I came to the Thailand camp. My new life in the Thailand camp was very hard. Sometimes I sewed clothes and sometimes planted a farm. I took care of my family.

When I first came here, my family was very sad. My children were wearing old clothes. I couldn't work. I have three children, but I didn't know how to take a bus or go to the grocery store.

Now I go everywhere, but I am not finding a good job. I wish I could, because I am learning new things in the school. My teacher teaches me to speak English and do homework. I try to go to school Monday through Friday, and now I know English better. I feel good, and someday I hope I will get a job.

The Worst Day of My Life 2009
Lillie K., Shakopee

The alarm was going off, the baby was crying, and my fiancé was lying cold on my arm. I tried to move him but he wouldn't wake up. I started screaming his name. My brother came running in and told me to call 911. He started doing CPR. At that moment, all I could hear was crying and screaming only to realize I was the one screaming. EMTs pronounced him dead on the scene. He had died three hours earlier.

Three months after his death, the police came to the door. My daughter and I were taking a nap and my son was at McDonald's. I was still sleepy when I answered, not realizing that my life was about to change forever. I found out the reason for my fiancé's death. He died of an overdose of methadone in the middle of the night. The methadone shut down his respiratory system. It was my methadone that killed him. I was placed under arrest for third degree murder; my children went to police holding.

At that time, my daughter was six months old and my son was 12. They had never been away from me. The police told me we had to go. I said, "Can we wait for my son?" I knew they would be scared. The police said no. As I was crying, I kissed my sleeping baby and wrote a note to my son, not knowing this would be the last time I would see home. When I arrived at the jail, as I lay there in my cell, a tear ran down my face. I asked myself what is happening? This is a nightmare, not knowing until now this would change my life forever.

This is My True Story
Ahmed Olol, Minneapolis

On September 28th, 2009, I experienced something I had never thought I would. I was living with my uncle. It was nearly midnight when my uncle heard knocking on our door. He asked, "Who are you?" The people who were knocking said, "We are police." Then my uncle opened the door. They entered and started to hit him badly. They knocked him into the wall and came toward me. At that moment, I was sleeping. I was not aware of what was going on in the room. They came up to me, and they started hitting me too. They even tore my left ear by hitting it. I wondered what kind of crime I did, because I had been in the United States for only five days.

They handcuffed me and prepared to take me to the station. I told them that I was new to this country and pointed at my documents. When they saw my documents, they said they were sorry. They were looking for someone else. They removed the handcuffs from my hands and left me bleeding.

I Missed My Wife
Abdikarim, Minneapolis

I was born in Mogadishu, the capital of Somalia. I have two brothers and two sisters. A civil war started in my country in 1991. I moved to Saudi Arabia. I missed my family and my friends. Saudi Arabia doesn't accept refugees. I couldn't live there, because I was a refugee. I moved to Switzerland, where they accepted me. My wife came to the United States in 1999 with her family. I didn't live with my wife for a long time because of the civil war. My wife sent me a visa and I moved to the USA. I live with my wife now. I have one kid. I have a good life now.

The Dangers of Three Wheelers
Mary Ommundson, Red Wing

I have had an experience with a three-wheeler. I had a bad accident with one when I was 21 years old. I got on it and started it and gave it a lot of gas. I lost control and hit a telephone pole. The three-wheeler came down on top of me. I was black and blue from my hip down. Two weeks later I went to the doctors and I had surgery. They put screws in my knees.

Now I am 37 years old, and I have had five knee surgeries and two hip surgeries. I have had my experiences with surgeries and I do not want to see a three-wheeler again. They are really dangerous. If you need to go on one, you need to know where everything is on it and wear a helmet.

Part of My Life
Mariana Pallazhco, Minneapolis

I am from Cuenca, Ecuador. When I was thirteen years old, I went to the city to work as a babysitter. After eight months, I moved to another city called Guayaquil. I was there working selling sodas, sandwiches, etc. I had my own business until I was 22 years old.

After that, I decided to come to the famous USA, which wasn't fun at all. It took me two months to get here. Before that, I got lost for seven days in the desert of New Mexico. It was in the summertime in August. The man who brought us left with our money. We were five people. We didn't have any water, no food, nothing. Finally, a man was walking by there, and he found us.

When I got to Brooklyn, New York, it was very different from what I had imagined when I was in my country. After three days, I went for my first day of work in a sewing factory which was something I'd never done. Oh God! That was the worst day of my life, because I'd never used those sewing machines. When I went back to my apartment, I cried a lot. I wanted to go back to my Ecuador, but I couldn't because at that time I owed money to my father and other people. It was about $8,000. That was in 1992. But over there, I learned that nothing was impossible because I learned how to use those machines. I practiced, and I learned a lot.

After that, I moved to Minneapolis, Minnesota, and I'm working in a flower shop as a flower designer and in customer service. I like it a lot. Thanks to God, so far everything is going okay. I have one daughter. She is twelve years old. She is my life.

I Remember 2003
Ngan Pham, Minneapolis

I am from Vietnam. I came to the USA almost ten years ago. I remember when I got a driver's license. I drove in the local area, not the freeway. But one day I drove on the freeway and I had an accident. I hit the motorcycle because I didn't see it behind me and I didn't know I hit him, so I drove and I drove. When I was nearby my house the taxi in front of my car stopped. The driver said, "You knocked out the motorcycle." I said I didn't know what happened. After I said this, I was nervous a lot because it was the first time I got in an accident and I didn't know how to speak English very well. Then I called my husband. The taxi driver called the police who gave me a ticket and he said, "You hit and ran," and he left.

The man who drove the motorcycle is my neighbor. He came and I asked him "How are you?" and he said, "I'm OK," and he wanted my money. I didn't give it to him. I said he should call his insurance company and I called mine, too. I went to court six times.

One month after the accident in the middle of the night, I got a phone call from Vietnam. My mom had a heart attack and was in the hospital. One week later, I had surgery in my ear and I stayed in the hospital one week.

After that, I never drove for six years. Right now I'm OK when I drive. That is my story that I remember from 2003.

My Real Life
Soukpaseut Keomany, Chanhassen

I was born in Laos. My life was very difficult, because my mom and dad were separated when I was five years old. I have one brother and one sister. I am the oldest. I had to help my mom. My country was Communist. It was very hard to live there at that time. My mom desired to escape to Thailand in 1979. At that time, I was a student. We had to stay in a refugee camp in Thailand for a year. Then my uncle sponsored my family to come to the US. We came on January 28, 1980. We lived in Columbus, Ohio for one year. Then we desired to move to Minnesota in 1981. We lived a lot of places.

In 1982, I got married. After thirteen years I ended up with a divorce. I hear people talking about the number thirteen as a bad number, an unlucky number. I believe it. I was married for thirteen years when that happened to my marriage. At that time my life was miserable. We had three kids together. I told my wife, "Can we make up?" I didn't want my three kids to end up like me when I was a little kid. I went to see a counselor to save my family. It still didn't work. I had no choice. I had to leave. As of right now we are very friendly—we understand each other and help each other. I am very happy. All my kids are grown up. They understand the situation. The United States is a very beautiful country to live in.

Wilma Griebel, Southern Minnesota

Telephone Problem
Mukhtar A Jimaleh, Minneapolis

When I came to the United States of America, it was very difficult for me to speak English or understand how to use the phone. If I called someone, nobody could understand what I wanted, and I didn't understand what they said.

I remember the first day I applied for a job in the United States of America. When I went to the job interview, my friend helped me. I wrote on the job application my cell phone number. After a few hours, when my friend left, they called me. Unfortunately, I couldn't understand. I got confused because I didn't know if she said "come to work

Struggles and Victories - 47

or not." However, when I missed my job at least three days, it caused misunderstanding. I looked for a solution and I decided, I wouldn't answer any phone, because I preferred messages. When they left a message, I found somebody to tell me what they said. Then when I knew the message's meaning, I repeated listening again and again for practice. It wasn't a solution really, but that time, it looked like a solution, in my opinion.

Therefore, I started school. I got better, and also I got the professional and experienced teachers in the Adult Education Schools. At my workplace, I got more practice. So I got better step-by-step.

Now, I am not perfect. But I am better by 70 percent. I understand most of them. I am using the phone very easily; I am working as a team leader. I am in charge of twenty people. I am using a radio, or "walkie-talkie." I am feeling very happy.

I never forget the American teachers, because they are professional and experienced people. They are helpful to me. I appreciate it, and I am saying thank you for your teaching.

Why Did I Cry?
Kemsrean Kheng, Minneapolis

The first day I got a new job in a company, I never worked like that before. I thought that I would be very happy, but I was unhappy. I worked so hard twelve hours a day. When I started the first day, I saw the supervisor. I felt very scared of him. When he asked me to do something, I only said yes and no. I felt upset because I can speak English a little bit. When I came back home, my mother always asked me about my job. I told her, "I don't like this job, but it is difficult for me to find another job in the United States. I don't want to work so hard. I always studied hard in Cambodia and Thailand. I graduated from the university and college. I didn't think I would come here, because I didn't have family and friends living here. I only studied the English a little bit. When the Cambodian Community Association invited me to come here, I felt so bad. It was too late to study English."

After my mother got my answer, she understood and was quiet. The second day I came back from working, she asked me again, "Are you tired today?" I answered her, "Yes, I'm so tired." At that time, she advised me about a lot of things. "You must think long and be patient before you quit this job," she said. "If you try hard you will get to be successful in the future. Don't forget my opinion."

> I have to be patient more than I ever did before. I hurt everything in my body.

I have to be patient more than I ever did before. I hurt everything in my body. That time, I was angry with her until I cried. One week, I went home from working and I got a swollen foot. Next day, I decided to stay home until my foot lost the swelling, then I went back working again. I began to think other people can do it too. I must to be patient; I worked so hard I didn't quit. For three months I worked hard on my job and communication. I must get a promotion and start making the tags.

This is my history. I just tell everybody we have to be patient so we get success. We must believe in ourselves. We must hope in our life. If we fall down we must get up to go on. We are working so hard. In the future, we will be working easy. This time we are poor people; next we are rich people.

Something I Regret
Nyanchew Donis, Coon Rapids

I wish I hadn't gotten married so young. I was engaged when I was sixteen. Part of my culture is that a girl can get married young—especially when she doesn't go to school. When I got engaged, I quit school, because people treated me like a woman already. That is not a good way to treat a young girl, because you miss your own personality. You don't want to disappoint your parents. Then you are afraid to do things the way you want to. The in-laws bully you when you want to talk to friends—even your cousin. You have to explain how you are related to that person. I wish I could take everything back. I would go to school even if it's hard. I would get a good job, a good car and a good house. I would take care of my family and me. Nobody would boss me. I would boss myself. Even so, God puts things the way they're supposed to be.

Nyanchew Donis is originally from Sudan.

The Current Darkness Which Led to a Bright Future
Anonymous, Minneapolis

I came to Minneapolis in 1994. It was during the summertime. All of my surroundings were green and sparkling with beautiful lakes. I felt that this country and my home had the same weather, but soon, the leaves started falling from the trees. One day, I asked my friend, "What's wrong with the trees?" She said that it was fall. My friend added that after fall, snow would come. I thought it would be fun and couldn't wait for the snow.

At the beginning of September, I started high school, because I was 17 years old. One day, the weather was normal, so I left my jacket and boots at home. That day, I got sick and my teacher sent me home. I didn't have someone to pick me up, so I went to the bus stop. My entire body was cold. When I got home, I had a fever. When my brother came home from work, he saw my condition and rushed me to the hospital immediately. A nurse gave me a painkiller and a doctor came in and examined me. He told us that I had pneumonia. He gave me medications that I would take for seven days, and after seven days I got better.

When I became an 18-year-old, I got married. After one month, I got pregnant with my first baby. One night, I woke up feeling a lot of pain, so I woke my husband and he took me to the hospital. After fifteen hours of labor, and a lot of pain, I gave birth to a baby girl. I told the nurse I didn't want to see the baby, because it caused me a lot of pain. I slept all night without seeing the baby.

At 11:00 a.m., a nurse said that I had to feed the baby, and I said, "OK!" The nurse gave me the baby and I fed her my milk. After that time, I started to love my daughter, and I still love her now. The reason why I refused to see her was that I was young and didn't have a mother to tell me how to love and care for a baby. From 1995 until 2008, I stayed at home and took care of my kids. I started at VOA, and I now know how to read and write English and how to communicate with people.

My Memory
Yurub Yusuf, Minneapolis

In 2003, I had a friend at school. I said something bad to my friend, and it was so bad I could understand why she was angry. I said I was sorry, but it was too late; she didn't forgive me.

On May 21st, she visited me at my home. It was a Friday afternoon and it was lunchtime. So we ate lunch, and then we went to the

Struggles and Victories - 49

fifth floor lounge so we could see people. But that is not what she really wanted. She had something else on her mind. I stood up and looked down. She came up behind me, grabbed my hands and held them behind my back. Then she pushed me to the ground. Someone shouted and I yelled for help. My leg was broken, my hand was broken, and my head was injured too.

My brothers rushed me to the hospital. I had blood everywhere. The family thought I would die. I was in a coma for fifteen days. The family was so sad, especially my mom. She cried more than you can imagine.

After fifteen days, I opened my eyes and the doctor called my family and told them the good news. Everybody in the family was so excited except my mom. She was happy to see me, but on the other hand there was bad news. The doctor talked to my mom and told her I was paralyzed.

My mom was in shock, and she could not remember what the doctor told her. But I was not paralyzed; I could feel my leg. I do not remember anything about what happened to me, but I was in the hospital for seven months.

In 2004, I started walking with a wheelchair. I was OK, but the big problem was to remember everything that used to be easy for me. It takes time to learn everything again, but in time I was walking. I thank Allah because I walk.

In 2005, we came to the US. Now my leg is fine and even my memory is fine. I learned a lesson to not say bad things to people.

The Earthquake
Farkhanda Sikandar, Maplewood

The earthquake in Haiti reminds me of the earthquake in Pakistan. In October 2006, a 7.8 earthquake happened in Pakistan. Everything shook and I felt like I was on a swing. It was Ramadan and we prayed all night. We were sleeping at the time of the quake. It was 9 o'clock in the morning. We ran so fast we weren't able to wear shoes. We screamed and cried. Everything was destroyed in front of my eyes. Nobody was there to help. People were under the rocks for weeks. Pakistani people helped each other. There are many people that are still homeless and they live in tents. That earthquake was a very bad disaster in my life. That few minutes was very bad for many, many people.

Poverty Story
Tou Vang Lee, Saint Paul

I was born in a refugee comp in Wathamkrabok, Thailand on June 24, 1989. I liked school but my mom and dad didn't have money to pay for the teachers, so I had to stay home with my brothers and sisters. Sometimes we played soccer in the street. We always cooked rice and a small fish. One day I asked my mom this question, "Mom, will you pay for the teachers and let me go to school?" She thought about it and said, "No, I can't let you go to school because you are the oldest brother, so I want you to work at home for your parents."

> Everything shook and I felt like I was on a swing. It was Ramadan and we prayed all night. We were sleeping at the time of the quake.

After that I did not say anything. I just did what she told me to do. Day after day, I thought and thought about school. I prayed by myself one day, "I will have school."

A few years later, the Hmong government said, the government of America wanted to take all of the Hmong people to the United States for freedom and education. When I heard that I was so happy. We had to wait for the government to call my parents' name. On November 24, 2004, we came to the United States.

I saw many beautiful things in the US. I started my education and began my life in the US. I go to school every day. I do my homework every night. I also get along with everybody. I got my driver's license on May 25, 2008. I am very happy to be here for freedom and education. For all of this, I think my life in America is great!

A Memory of My Childhood
Abeba Shashego, Richfield

I am not sure about my age—I think I was nine years old. It is difficult for a young child to hear about war, violence, rebellion, etc. Here is my story that happened when I was young.

The story begins from the world at that time. I think there was war in Iraq. The president of Iraq, Saddam Hussein, was a dictator and said that "we should destroy the world by a nuclear bomb." I heard these words on our little radio every day. Even people were talking about these things, and that made me very disturbed. I was worried about the situation, but I didn't tell anyone. One day, when I woke up in the morning, I wondered if we were alive. I thought we were dying from a nuclear bomb that was shot from Iraq. I said to my mom, "We are not dead!"

And she asked, "What happened?"

I told her about my feeling about the war and the nuclear bomb. "Will the bomb destroy us? Why don't we flee to another place?" I thought that was a better idea to run away from the bomb.

But she said to me, "Nobody is hurting or killing you. Who said that?"

I said, "Everybody is taking about this."

She said, "Don't be afraid. This doesn't concern us, just forget it." At that moment, I felt better. My mom was feeling guilty about my situation because she was reminded that talking and listening to bad things in front of children's faces is not good. After all that passed, I remembered the situation and what I thought about my childhood memory.

The War
Cher Her, Oakdale

I remember when I was a child, my grandfather told me about the Vietnam War. In 1960 to 1975 in Laos, many people had problems from the Vietnam War. During this time, people died from fighting and it was a hard time for people to live in the country. All the men age fifteen years old and up had to go to the war. In some villages, the soldiers came and killed people, so many families lost their husband and wife. At that time, the children did not have the opportunity to go to school. The people did not know when the war ended. I remember many things my grandfather told me in the past. Now in my home country it is better than during the war.

Cher Her is originally from Laos.

A Severe Earthquake Destroyed Port-au-Prince
Claudy, North Saint Paul

I am from Haiti. Haiti is a Caribbean country, and its capital is Port-au-Prince. The total population of Haiti is around 9 million people. Haitian Creole and French are the official languages. On January 12th, 2010, I received a phone call from my wife; it was about six o'clock p.m., and at that time, I was at school, so I didn't pick up the call. However, she left me a voice message, and I waited until the class was done to listen to it. She called me just to let me know about the earthquake that struck Haiti. When I got home, I turned on the TV to CNN and watched how my country was destroyed. The magnitude of the earthquake was 7.0 with its epicenter 16 miles from the capital, Port-au-Prince, the largest city—all was devastated. At least 200,000 people were dead, albeit it will take time to determine the exact number of the dead. However, one person jumped from the sixth floor of a school and survived. She was my sister! Many important structures such as the Presidential Palace and the Parliament were destroyed, along with countless homes, businesses, hospitals, schools, churches, and shanty towns. This earthquake is the country's most severe in two centuries. At this moment, the entire world is focused on Haiti.

In my opinion, this earthquake is a message from God for the Haitian people. They have to unite as the motto of Haiti says: "Unity is strength," and it is time for them to show that strength and unity. The message is not only for Haiti, but it is for the entire world. I am glad that a lot of countries, such as the United States of America, Canada and Europe, put their hands together to save lives in Haiti, because today is for Haiti, but we don't know who else might be affected in the future.

Untitled
James Williams, Maplewood

I grew up in the streets of causalities
From principalities.
Yet I
Battled these with diligence,
And relentlessness,
As I made my pilgrimage to a new land
Where your two cents was proof
That you were a nuisance or a scholar.
See, there was this lady
Who had a dream
That her seed would succeed,
And bred in the same likeness
I like this, her aspiration
I am her seed, and with patience I made this possible,
Something or someone so minute made so colossal
My ancestor's fossils were not in vain,
Cause as the world turns,
I learn that this little light of mine I burn as though a candle,
By the footprints of my sandals,
I walk this lonely road the only road I have ever known,
From a neophyte till I was grown,
I was prone to this woman's virtues
And her husbands learnt dues,
As I swallowed up the knowledge of the world,
Like cooked foods,
I am a fine tree with deep roots
Yes these are my streets
This is my struggle
And no I would not
Should not
And could not fail
Here I am legend

James Williams is 25 years old.

Me and My Family
Hussein Ali, Fridley

My name is Hussein Ali, and I was born in Hargesa, Somalia in 1986. I have two brothers. My father had two wives. My older brother had another mother, and my sister had the same mother. My older brother was born in Mogadishu. My father was married to my mother. When my mother and my father married, they moved to Hargesa because my father was in the military. The government transferred him to Hargesa in 1984. After one year, my sister was born. Her name is Hamdi. My father died in May 1986, two months before I was born. I never saw my father's face or what he looked like.

When the Somali Civil War started, my cousin sent a message to my mom telling her to bring us to him so we would be safe. My cousin was living in Djibouti. My auntie said that she would take us to Djibouti. I was three years old that day. My auntie put me on her back. I was crying and my mom was also crying. My brother wanted my auntie to take the car, but she refused and said she would walk instead. One day later, my auntie saw the car, which someone else had taken, and it was burning. Finally we came to Djibouti. When I grew up, my uncle sponsored my family to come to the U.S., but my mom, my brother, and my sister refused. My auntie and I came to the United States on April 6th, 2007 and we started a new life. I miss my family.

My First Phone Call
Charlene Litchke, Minneapolis

When I first came to this country from Salvador, Brazil, it was very difficult for me to use the phone. I didn't speak English. To talk with people was hard for me, but listening to them on the phone was almost impossible. My first experience was with my mother-in-law, who is from America. She asked me, "How are you?" and I answered with the one sentence I knew in English: "I'm fine, and you?" In that moment she started to talk English very fast, and I only said, "Casey, Casey, Casey"—my husband's name.

My hardest problem using the phone was when people left messages for me. They didn't speak slowly and expected that I could understand everything. I always listened to the messages more than four times to practice my English.

> My hardest problem using the phone was when people left messages for me.

Every day, I became more comfortable using the phone. I appreciate it when people call me, and we have good conversations.

I Remember...
Ana Santos, Saint Cloud

Twenty-nine years ago, when I was 6 years old, somebody went to my parents' house. They were very bad people called "Guerrilleros," and they started to knock the door until they broke the door and they killed our dog. After that, they took my dad outside the house. Then they told him it will be the last time he saw his family. My dad started to hug everyone, and then he left. After about two hours, we heard when the bad people went back on the road, and my mom decided to go look around to try to find my dad. We found he was dead. They killed him.

I Almost Died

This is what happened to me when I was 5 years old. My family and I were living in Kenya. We went back to Somalia to learn our culture. At that time the Civil War in Somalia hadn't started yet. After a year had passed, the war started. We ran from our home in Mogadishu to my uncle's home in Kambo Amaxar.

One night, around 6 p.m., I was playing with some cats outside in front of my uncle's house. When my uncle came outside to pray Maqrib he said to me, "Safiyo, go inside. It's getting dark out here." My uncle went on his way to pray. I didn't listen to my uncle; I kept playing with the cats. After a few minutes passed, someone shot a gun, right at my head. Luckily it didn't go all the way in or break my skull.

I started running and shouting, "Mom! Mom!" I thought my uncle had poured hot water on me because the blood from my head had run onto my shoulder and it was so warm. I started running around and around my mother who was standing there. It was dark so no one knew what had happened to me. Finally, my uncle's wife got a light and what they saw they could not believe.

Safiyo Mohamed Osman is 23 years old and a student at VOA Adult High School. She came to the United States nine years ago from Kenya and now lives in Minneapolis with her husband, Mustafa, and their two kids, Abdinasir age two years and Zaidan age six months.

She enjoys listening to all types of music, likes to spend time with her family and friends, and also enjoys playing soccer and video games with her husband and kids. Insha Allah, after high school she wants to get a college degree so she can have a professional career.

My First Time to the United States
Roman Worku, Minneapolis

I came to the USA on May 12, 2006. When I came to the Unites States, I lived with my sponsor. I started my new life. My new life was very difficult, because my sponsor and his family were very busy. I was really scared, because I didn't know how to take the bus or find a job.

After three months, I went to school. I tried to speak to different people for help getting a job. One lady told me a lot of people find jobs at the airport. I did find a job at the airport. I was really happy!

My first job was very easy, but I didn't like it, because my co-workers spoke the same language. There is no opportunity to learn English that way.

I would like to get a better job. Then I will have a better life and be able to go back to Ethiopia to join my husband.

World Peace
Hui Ying Chen, Owatonna

I was living in New York City on September 11th, 2001. It was a day of terror when the twin towers were hit by the airplanes, so many people lost members of their families.

That morning, I was sleeping when it happened. I couldn't believe my eyes that this was true. That day, the traffic was stopped and no one was going anywhere.

I heard many people crying because they were broken-hearted. I hope this never happens again, and I wish for world peace.

Hui Ying Chen is 37 years old and is originally from China Fu Jian.

The Impact of War
Garnary Doe, Brooklyn Park

Are you acquainted with war? Country against country, insurgents against government. It is something terrifying that you don't want to experience. The world is surrounded by destructive people. The news reports about wicked, evil, unmerciful people that are causing problems every day. I weep when I see these bad things on the news. I have been an eyewitness to it in my country, Liberia.

My name is Garnary Doe. I was born in Monrovia, Liberia, West Africa. I have four brothers and three sisters. Liberia was a land of peace, a beautiful country with ocean, lakes, rivers, and other natural resources. As a little boy, I never knew about traveling and didn't consider it. My family was my pride. They treated me like a baby, but I received punishment when I disobeyed.

In December 1990, the country was informed that rebels were in the northeastern part. I asked my mother, "How long will it last? What impact will it have on the country? Are we going to leave our home? Where will we go?" She didn't answer my questions, but later she said, "We have to pray."

After a few months, things started to change. The fighting escalated to the city. Food became scarce. Drinking water and electricity were in short supply. By June, things were really bad. War brings the opposite of development. Instead it results in economic breakdown, destruction, and seeking refuge in another country. We had to relocate to a safer place.

Our destination was the next city, called Bushrod Island. It is surrounded by a large body of water. To get there, we started to walk, but the journey was too far. It was the first long walk I had ever experienced. As we continued to walk, I saw some dreadful things that a little boy like me should never have to see. Dead bodies were lying along the side of the street. Burned buildings, burned cars, and bullet shells were everywhere. I was tired, hungry, and even thirsty, but I had no options.

Eventually, we made our way onto a ship that was going to Ghana. The Ghanaian government placed the Liberians in a camp near the city called Accra. We lived in Ghana for years before immigrating to the United States of America. Thank God for his blessings.

The Horrible Way Home
Kayoua Faust, Hugo

During 1998 in the middle of January, my third month living in the United States, I got my first job. The company was on the opposite side of the city. At that time, I did not speak English and I wasn't driving a car so I took a bus to work. The bus had to transfer between home and work.

When I got onto the first bus, I was so tired and wanted to sleep. I tried to keep myself awake before the bus stopped to transfer. I was so sleepy and I could not control it, my head kept nodding off of my seat. On the first bus, I was okay, but on the second, I fell asleep until the bus stopped at the station.

When the bus driver came to wake me up, I was the only one on the bus and I did not speak any English. I thought to myself, "How can I get back home and how far had I gone past my stop?" I was so scared because I didn't speak English so I could not ask any questions. I did not know what to do and which bus I should take to get back home. I tried to ask him for help, but he could not understand me.

He showed his ID to me and I gave him mine. He smiled at me and then he beckoned me to follow him. It was good timing; he found one African-American woman who lived near me. After he talked to the lady she held my arm to go with her that made me feel better.

We waited for the next bus for thirty minutes in the frigid weather. We got onto the bus, later she rang a bell for the driver to stop at my house. Before I left, I said thank you to her in my language and hopefully she understood me. Eventually I got home from work, but it took three hours. Usually it took forty-five minutes.

After that I never fell asleep on the bus anymore. I wish that I could find the bus driver and the African-American woman. I would like thank them again for helping me and making me feel better. Because back then I could not say any words in English to them and that made me feel so sad.

Kayoua Faust is originally from Laos.

America is a Good Place for a Widow with Children
Fadumo Ali, Saint Paul

I was born on March 2nd, 1975 in Somalia. I came to the States on May 16th, 2000. My husband died in 2005. I had a bad time this year because I was alone with four children. When he died, I was six months pregnant. I delivered a new baby girl. Right now, I feel better because America is very good to me and my children.

Paralysis of the Vocal Chords
Erika Serrano, Waite Park

On April 30th, when my older son was born, I was so happy. But the doctors noticed that something was not right. When he swallowed, he would get purple and start to choke. So the doctors rushed him to the hospital in Minneapolis. It was a very difficult experience.

I was twenty years old without my side of the family here with me. After ten days staying in the hospital in Minneapolis, the doctors gave me great news on my birthday. The doctors determined my son could go home with us, but he needed a machine that would monitor his heartbeat.

I had to breastfeed him in a certain position for eight months. Also, the first six months, he got high fevers and seizures after his fever went up. All this happened because the lateral vocal cord was paralyzed, with time his vocal chord came to life. My son was out of danger. I thanked the Lord God because I had prayed and cried a lot. I didn't want to see my little son suffer. I said thanks many times, because not all kids had the same faith or miracle.

There is not a school that teaches you how to be a mother, but life experiences help you resolve problems. You can either fall or not face your problems, or you learn to resolve them. My hope and faith are the things that I needed to see the past through.

There is no greater fortune and grace than to be a mother.

Erika Serrano is originally from Mexico.

Experience the New World
Zareen Zafar, Rosemount

I have been in Minnesota for the last three years. I like to live in Minnesota. I have moved to many cities, so I had a chance to meet many people and have many interesting experiences.

The first time I came to the USA, for me many things were very good, and many things were very strange. In New York—in the beginning—I was terrified because some people told me that I should not trust anyone, because there many people were robbed and some were killed. So, my first impression was that because of differences in culture, maybe we were not protected and safe in all parts of the USA.

When we moved to New Hampshire, there was an incident that changed my views. One day, I had to get some groceries from a store at night. After I got my groceries, I came back to my car and tried to start my car, but I couldn't start my car. My key was stuck. Meanwhile, an old man parked his car in front of my car and went into the store. My cell phone battery was low, so I could not call any of my friends. The parking lot was empty too. I was praying in my heart to Allah and confused about what I should do. Then that old man came to my car and noticed that I was upset. "Do you need any help?" he asked.

I was confused, and thought, "Should I trust a stranger or not?"

> I decided to trust him and told him about my problem. He checked my car and solved the problem. I thanked him.

I decided to trust him and told him about my problem. He checked my car and solved the problem. I thanked him.

I realized that when Allah sends people to this world, they are all innocent and good. But when they grow up, sometimes their environment makes them bad. Still, many people don't change their original good nature. So, if we have to go anywhere, like Africa, an Asian country or the USA, we

Struggles and Victories - 57

might meet some bad people, yet we should not think that all people of that country are bad and evil. We can find bad and good people everywhere, and I am lucky that Allah has sent me to places where I found mostly good people and very few bad people. Minnesota is one of those places.

Zareen Zafar is 40 years old and is originally from Pakistan.

A Survivor in Laos
Hlee Thao, White Bear Lake

I do not remember how old I was when I still lived in Laos. The war was going on in 1975. My family was living in Laos. We had many hardships, because we had no place to stay. We were hiding in the jungle, running from mountain to mountain from the Communist regime. I remember being so hungry. We had no food to eat. We had no rice, meat, or salt, but we did have some green beans left to support the family. One day, my mom was so worried that all the beans would be eaten, then we would not have anything left to eat, so my mom took me with her to find some potatoes in the jungle. We found some potatoes, but they were very bitter. Even though it tasted bad, we had no choice but to eat it, otherwise we would have died from hunger. I am very lucky that my mom and I do not have to go find bitter potatoes again, because we ended up in the United States. We live in nice homes and have a lot of food to support the family. We do not run anymore.

Rebecca's Story
Rebecca Jock, Owatonna

I am from Sudan and belong to the Nur people. I was born in 1982. My father was a Christian fighting against the Northern forces of Sudan who were Muslim. I lived with my mother and older sister in Nasir, Sudan. My father traveled back and forth to our home as he fought in the war. We lived over two years in a refugee camp, and my mother was a leader who distributed food. There was a lot of fighting between the Nur people. My mother took my sister to Kartum for medical care. I held my little brother, telling him not to cry because they would kill us. My three uncles were killed by guns in front of us. In the morning, we saw dead bodies lying everywhere.

Because I was a child alone in a refugee camp, I got forms from the United Nations to request leaving Sudan for America. It was very hard because I didn't speak English. After one month, I left for the United States. I had no idea I was pregnant. I came to the United States on June 9th, 1999, without any family. I lived in Dallas, Texas for three weeks with a good sponsor, Mara Boss, who was good to me and told me many things about America.

I moved to Omaha to be closer to other

Har Rom, Saint Paul

Nur people. I had my daughter on February 27th, 2000. I had no one to help me. When Nyakhor was six weeks old, I began working at Tyson Meat Company. When I started there, they provided me an interpreter who could show me what to do. I worked and sent money every month to support my brother and my sister.

I had experienced several domestic situations, where I called the police for protection. My family has given guidance and support. After a time, I moved to Owatonna. I've met some people who are supportive of me. On December 1st, 2009 I passed my citizenship exam and am looking forward to my swearing-in ceremony on January 20th, 2010. I want to study more, get a good education and get a better job. I want to be strong and independent and above all, take good care of my children. I don't want to ever forget where I came from, about Africa and my people.

Rebecca Jock is 27 years old and is originally from Sudan.

Civil War
Fadumo Ali, Minneapolis

Before the Civil War started, we had a government. Also, our country was a peaceful country. But now, we have no peace and our people are dying without reason. The problem of our Civil War was tribalism. It is very bad and has no cure. Somalia is divided into many groups. Each group was killing in order to loot their property. At that time, many people died and people fled from Somalia to neighboring countries like Ethiopia and Kenya. Some of them died on the way, and some of them ate wild animals like lions and snakes. Soon some of them suffered on the way with hunger and thirst, because they ran from property and their enemies were hunting them. My family and I (except my brother, who was killed) fled to Kenya. We didn't bury his body, because a lot of bodies were lying on the ground. No one was interested in any dead bodies because everyone was scared and running for their lives.

Many of my relatives took a boat from Kismayo to Mombasa. It was a very, very big boat, but people were overcrowded. I didn't know the number of people who were on the boat, but there were many people. When the boat reached Kenyan seawater, it broke into two pieces. The boat sank into the sea upside down and many people died, except for a few people who knew how to swim. Six hundred people died at the same time. I know a man whose nine children and his wife died at one time and also his father-in-law, his wife, and his five children. That boat was the biggest accident in our Civil War. Many boats sank at sea. Unfortunately, Somali people still are fighting. Some of them don't want any government, because they learned how to kill people and how to loot their property. Many times, world governments have helped the Somali people and built a couple of governments, but the people who looted houses, farms, cars and trucks also looted the property of the last government and still they are looking for more to loot. We asked our God to take them from the world.

Earthquake
Manuel Contreras, Maplewood

Earthquakes are a serious and natural disaster. Not only do they hurt people, but they destroy infrastructures like buildings, roads, and field crops. They can also shatter the soul. All the time, we had earthquakes, but now that there is better communication like radio, telephone, Internet, (satellite, TV), we know the news quickly. For example, in Haiti some messages saved lives using cell phones. We now know in a few minutes about the earthquake because the TV was key. Right now, the technology is very important and advanced. The physical aspect of Haiti is impressive, because we see the destruction and the political leaders requesting great support from the world. They have received tremendous response!

In conclusion, I feel powerless to manage this problem; however I can help send money to the country.

Manuel Contreras is originally from El Salvador.

My Plan
Bla Vang, Minneapolis

In my future, I plan to move far from the city. However, I would like to get my citizenship and find a job so I will get more money to buy a new house. Now I have a house in the city, but this house is in a noisy neighborhood, and people dislike cleaning their place in my neighborhood. I saw people throw garbage everywhere on the street, yard and around the rear of the house. Sometimes I do not feel safe for my family. If I have a chance or money, I would like to buy a house far from the city.

Intercom
Kay Cox, Minnetonka

When I first came to the United States, my husband and I lived in Denver, Colorado. We lived in an apartment that had a security door at each entrance, and if someone from outside wanted to talk to residents, they had to use the intercom to call that apartment.

One day, my husband and I were at home and someone at the front security door called our intercom. Sometimes sales people came by and tried to sell magazines, so I thought that might be the situation. I was trying to say "no thank you," but I didn't speak much English then. I always tried to avoid conversation with strangers, too. When someone rang our intercom that day, I answered. The voice said he had a package for me. I didn't understand what that meant, so I told the person no thank you and I turned off the intercom. My husband approached the intercom fast, and I didn't understand why, but I found out soon. He told the man he would be right there, and he told me that it was the postman at the door, not a salesperson. I was so embarrassed, and I didn't know what to say. After that incident, I didn't answer the intercom anymore.

Mistakes
Yosef Baji Patrick, Rochester

Life is a big mistake. Not saying that we are a mistake for God creating us, but a learning process that's caused by mistakes. For some of us, we learn from our mistakes and try our hardest not to make them again, or should I say, repeat them. On the other hand, some of us just seem to be caught up in our mistakes and that makes it harder for us to correct them or overcome them. Sometimes it's hard for us to recognize them or even admit that we've made a mistake. Some mistakes we make turn into great opportunities, but that's very rare. Without a foe, a soldier never knows his strength, so when we make mistakes in life, we learn the better way of doing things and also learn how to make the right decisions in life. At the same time, they increase our awareness level. In other words, mistakes can have good and bad outcomes. What we do, or should I say, how we respond, will determine the overall outcome.

About My Living in Somalia
Anonymous, Minneapolis

I was born in 1986, in the capitol city of Somalia. When I was five years old, I went to Dugsi, which means "Islamic school." Unfortunately, a few months later, the civil war erupted, and I had a very hard time. This motivated me to run to the neighbor country, the one they call Kenya. My family was sad and worried about how they could get in, because they didn't have any ID. I didn't care about what was going on because of my age. The family began to talk to the people who lived in a city in the border area. However, somehow we got in that country. As soon as we got in, we met some people crowded and lined up to get temporary papers. Finally, the entire family got papers. Those papers allowed them to enjoy Kenyan refugee camps. My family felt safe and received welcome with open hands from the Kenyan people. My family says thanks for their welcome.

A Refugee in Minnesota
Sewanta Adhikari, Saint Paul

I was born in a small, beautiful country, Bhutan. My family is poor. The situation of my country got worse and worse. There was a tyrannical government, so all the people were dominated, women were exploited sexually, many people were put in jail for decades and were discriminated harshly on the basis of castes, language, religion and clothing too. Eventually, people could not tolerate such tortures, and people were compelled to leave the country. When I left my country, I was an infant. That was approximately nineteen years ago. We all went to Nepal and stayed there as refugees.

My life in the refugee camp was so difficult because I had to live with the benefits which were provided by organizations such as WFP and CARITAS, etc. My life in the refugee camp was very scary, sad and unsafe. I was given five kilograms of rice for fifteen days, but unfortunately, it lasted for only ten days. Sometimes I had to face famine.

At any cost, I had to live my life, so I started going to school when I was five. My first day at school was not good because I was alone and I was feeling bored. But after some days, I started making friends at school. That year, I made much progress. I was so excited to go to college, but I could not because I had no money. Meanwhile, I got an opportunity to teach in the Boarding School. I taught in many schools, and I had a good reputation there.

Fortunately, I got a chance to come to the US through a Refugee visa in August 2009. Now, I am excited to make new friends and have fun with them. My life is absolutely different in America than in the refugee camp. I am happy to be in Minnesota with my family.

My Life
Fauzia Shawich Tia, Andover

My name is Fauzia Shawich Tia. I was born in Khadukle, Sudan, January 1st, 1971. I went to school up to the seventh grade. I was married in 1985 and had my first son in December 1986. I worked with children with nutritional needs in Khartoum from 1991 to 1994, when I left to Port Sudan. After my husband left the country and joined the Southern Sudan Rebel Movement (SPLA), the security forces started coming to my house, questioning me. I lied to them and told them he went to Port Sudan to visit my elder brother and he would be back soon, since they threatened to take my children if he did not come back.

Immediately, I took a train to Port Sudan

with my children and my husband's younger brother. I found my elder brother waiting with a message from my husband that we had to leave to Eritrea and meet him there.

I was nine months pregnant with my fourth child when I left Khartoum, and my daughter was born immediately upon arrival, so we stayed for two weeks. The security was very tight everywhere, especially at the border. We traveled at night, avoiding the highway and going in the forest. I was carrying my newborn wrapped in a blanket and my husband's brother was carrying my third youngest daughter. We traveled three days on foot while avoiding capture by Moralin (nomadic Arabs) who can make us their slaves. We arrived at the border and met my husband, who helped us across. We went to immigration and registered and were turned over to the UN, transported to Asmara, the capital of Eritrea, and taken to the refugees' camp. The journey was really difficult. We were scared by wolves and other animals, but after we arrived to Eritrea, I felt the journey was worth it. We felt safe, and we began our refugee resettlement process to the United States. We finally came here in 1999.

I started school here in the United States in 1999 to learn English and to become a US citizen. I take breaks from my schooling when I have my children, but have always gone back when I am able to continue my education. I started work for Head Start in January 2001. I work with teachers and children as a classroom aide. I would like to achieve a CDA to become an Assistant Teacher.

Where's My Baby?
Akwata Lero, Mankato

The year after I came to America, I found out I was pregnant. We were going to have twins! My husband was happy, but I was crying all the time. My aunt had two sets of twins. I had to help take care of them, and it was a lot of work.

After a hard pregnancy, I had the babies, but I couldn't see them for a day. Then I asked for them. When they brought them, one baby's face was all red and bruised. I thought they had changed my baby for someone else's! I told them, "That is not my baby. Bring this baby back and bring my baby to me."

They didn't understand what I was trying to say. They thought maybe I only wanted one baby, and I didn't want the other one.

I called my husband at home. He came and said, "It's our baby." They sent a doctor and nurse to tell me about the wrist band, how the number on my wristband and on the baby's is the same number, so it's my baby.

They made me stay in the hospital for five days because I couldn't breastfeed them both at the same time. I could only do one at a time. After five days, I came home. I didn't know how to change a diaper. We don't have them in Sudan. I tried to put it on so it doesn't touch the cord, but it didn't work. Pee went everywhere!

I had a friend and neighbor from Mexico. She came and showed me how to do it. There was no one from my family or even from my country.

I was tired all the time. I had to cook for five people every day. It was really hard. Now the twin boys are 12 and they help me.

Yemen and the U.S.
Khadija Adan, Marshall

My name is Khadija Adan. On October 6th, 1991, I escaped out of Somalia to Yemen. Then I was put in jail for four months. I didn't have any documents to enter Yemen. After that, I got a refugee card. Then I came to Aden City. I was looking for a job. I got a

Being Locked Up
Keith June Year, Duluth

Being locked up is you all alone
Waking up wishing you were home
Being locked up is a waste of time
Makes you think twice about the crime
Being locked up just makes you wonder

Anger
EJ, Duluth

Today is a day I'm mad at the world
I woke up so early that I almost hurled
I'm mad that my breakfast wasn't what I liked
I'm furious the milk was warm, and I think it was spiked
I hate the daily grind; I'm sick of the routine
I'm tired of hard labor, if you know what I mean
I'm irritated with the drivers when I'm on my way home
I want to hop out and bash their heads on my chrome
I'm sick of the nagging when I walk through the door
I'm enraged by the toys that are still on the floor
I'm annoyed I have to do dishes and also mow the lawn
But I've done so much complaining that my anger…is gone!

Grow
Samson Waddell, Duluth

It's funny how time passes.
I know when the going becomes rough
one must recognize the changes.
Suspend time, breathe,
so your restless soul could be revived.
Hey, take time to laugh, and a moment for tears.
Count all blessings continuously keeping something.
Everyone gravitates to the perfect atmosphere.
While growing we discover peace,
we find joy a beautiful experience.

In This Cage
Paul Christopher Hanninen, Superior

In this cage they claim now different.
In this cage where today I am living.
In this cage and all is giving.
In this cage that brings me rage.
In this cage I feel not forgiven.
In this cage to pace back and forth.
In this cage to wonder what's it's for.
In this cage I taste its worst.
In this cage all death not birth.
In this cage that keeps me reeling.
In this cage I hope for nothing.

Whispering Wind
Jayson Knutson, Bemidji

Whispering wind,
always so violent
but at times so tame.
Whispering wind,
what do you try to say,
changing as often as night
and day.
Whispering wind,
that never stays.
Whispering wind,
that I hear,
always a whistle,
in my ear.
"O" Whispering wind,
sing your violent song,
for soon the storm,
will go away.
You'll have no more to say…

A Letter to My Great Grandchildren

Hello to everyone. I am glad to see all of your smiling faces. Let's get started on my journey to a very happy place. I am going to get my GED and go to college to get a Master's degree in Computer Administration and Repair. This is one of my goals even if it takes me a lifetime to do. I will take the steps I need to get there, even though it means there is a lot of work to be done.

First is to get past the obstacles that are trying to stop me from getting my GED. I had two aneurysms. Now I have to learn to get all of the things that I know back in writing so you can see how I have come back the way granny was before the aneurysms. I have to learn to put it back on record so that you can still see me in a better light to help you accomplish things that I had done up to now. Now I want to accomplish the things that I have helped you to accomplish. I want my GED, and a college degree and a Master's degree. So you will know how important it is for you to stay in school and make your mark in life for you and your children's children. First thing for me to do is to make a list that has stopped me from achieving what I want to do. People with negative attitudes need to stay away, because this is the year for me to shine like a beacon of light that is going to keep floating on.

Love, Granny

My name is Alvester Morman. I am a 60-year-old African-American mother, grandmother, great-grandmother of five. I have an identical twin sister. I was born to Louis and Juanita Morman in Grace, Mississippi. I live in Minneapolis and I came back to school at Northside ABE to get my GED and prepare for college. In my free time, I like to crochet, work on the computer, do crafts with my great-grandchildren, and go to the museums and parks.

Life Decisions
Ariane Ferreira, Shakopee

Deciding to live in another country
Is a hard decision
For some of us it's good, for others not
But most have a good reason for

Leaving family, friends, and everything
Trying all new
Looking to improve ourselves
Looking for a new view

I'm thankful for the new friends
Thankful for the new place
Thankful for all the knowledge
And thankful that my family is still safe

Thank God for opening all the doors
For the good people I have met here
And I pray for the people who
Haven't had the same luck as me

I left my country one year ago
Looking back at me
I see how much I grew up
And I'm looking forward to how much waits for me

Ariane Ferreira is 22 years old and is originally from Brazil.

Life
Jacob Solberg, Duluth

The life I live is so full of sorrow
The life I live—is there gonna be a tomorrow?
Yet I know the life I live will be so sweet
The life I live will be so elite

Lights Out
Wesley Watts, Saint Paul

Searching for constellations
On the ceiling of a jail cell
But thus far no stars
Just fluorescent bulbs shining
Giving improper meaning to "lights out"
And it's easier to start believing God is with you
Because there's nothing else to spark up hope
And through the dreams I float
Like a smoke cloud slowly through the air of heaven
Then wake up into a living hell
Made of concrete and rebar
Some are demons and some have heart
Some are lost and some are found
But I just feel like a witness
Searching for forgiveness
Begging for a breath of fresh air
While I am searching for constellations
On the ceiling of a jail cell.

Sleepless Night
Michael Bailor, Saginaw

Sleepless night where neither rest nor morning
Will come up revising, reliving the events of the past days
Oh, sleepless night, how much I have lost
Each second passes, but still no relaxing, calming or tired sensation
Mind filled with endless thought and pointless worry
Of future time that not yet exists
Oh, sleepless night, with no supplication
How long will you last?
Oh, sleepless night, emotional deprivation that spans
Deep into the vastness of this old, oh sleepless night

housekeeping job. I worked about three-and-a-half years. Then I was in jail again for one month, because I lost my new card. The UN gave a card to me.

In 1998, I got a visa. When I came to the United States in 1999, I didn't speak English. I couldn't even read or write it. Also I didn't understand people when they asked me questions. I became nervous and shy. Then I tried to go to the ESL class. My first teacher was so nice. Her name is Lela Chacon. I will never forget her. I said, "Thank you so much."

One day I asked her, "When will I understand English?" She told me in a few days. Also she encouraged me to keep going to class. However, I got different teachers. They helped me so much and I succeeded in learning to speak English. In 2006, I became a United States citizen.

In conclusion, I want to thank all my teachers and the U.S. in general and the state of Minnesota in particular for their efforts to help me become who I am.

Fighting in Mugadisho
Anonymous, Minneapolis

One day when I was 8 years old, my family and I were staying at home. We were enjoying ourselves with my brother. He came from Eritrea and he was visiting us. We heard a noise that came from around the city. We were confused. After twenty minutes, we saw the bullets hit the people and the buildings. We were worried about our lives. So we took some food and clothes and etc., and left the city. We rode on a truck to the forest. We lived there in several nights under a tree. After that, we decided to move to Ethiopia. When we came to Ethiopia, we felt exhausted and we also felt unhappy because we left our home and our country. Then a few months later, we moved to Kenya. After that, we came back to normal, and we forgot about the past. I don't remember it at all but I try to think some of it. That is a little thing to write today.

Yesterday, Today, and Tomorrow
Elliott Williams, Saint Cloud

Just yesterday, I was a kid running and having fun, living life with no cares. Just yesterday, I had no fear. I dreamed of becoming a lawyer or becoming rich and having a family. Just yesterday, everything changed, now I'm running with a gang trying to chase fame, feeling nothing but pain. Just yesterday, I lost control of my life, sitting in this cell with no lights, lost with no hopes or dreams. Just yesterday, I was free, living life like a king. I wish it was yesterday; I would start over and follow my dreams.

Tomorrow is not promised, but for me tomorrow is promised because tomorrow for me will be better than today. Tomorrow is freedom, one more step toward understanding life. In my tomorrow, today will be the past. Today, I was the student, but tomorrow I will be the teacher. When I lived yesterday I gave up, today I tried, and tomorrow I will know success. You locked me down and talked about me, but I still found a way to be on top and free. Don't come around, because no matter what you do you can't bring me down. Yesterday and today you told me that I couldn't make it and that I would never be anything but a thug and die in the streets, but you just made me stronger. Tomorrow has become my today, and as you can see, I am a product of my community. I'm a man that tomorrow is promised to. Tomorrow is my future.

Today I thank God for today, because yesterday today was not promised. Today I become better than I was yesterday. Today I stop feeling guilty about sitting in this cell, and I stand up and start believing and stop hoping and start doing. I can't take back what

I did yesterday, but I can change what I do today. Today I will learn more about myself and about others. I will not give up. I am not a boy anymore. Today I'm a man. Today I will not look down on the past. I will not live in pain or with pain, and I will not give out pain because today I'm a man. Today is a new beginning. Today I develop; tomorrow I will become.

Pill Poem
Nick Whitman, Cotton

Went to the doctor; told him I felt blue
He gave me some pills; told me they were new
The ones he handed me were called Prozac
A few weeks later my blues turned to black
The next we tried were called Effexor
But three times a day soon became a chore
He re-diagnosed me and said I was bipolar
Said what would work is a good stabilizer
Lithium was the one we tried first
But I couldn't tolerate my unquenchable thirst
Another one we tried was named Depakote
Pretty soon I wanted to slit my throat
Switched to another, it was Wellbutrin
A waste of time soon to me it was proven
Then it was one; I think it was Seroquil
I slept very well, but it made me feel ill
I realized soon I wasn't out of my mind
And taking these pills was a waste of my time

Moments of Time
Samuel L Porter, Duluth

As the clock slowly turns its hands
Minutes and hours, day to day
Working on the job collecting pay
Thinking of more making business plans
Weeks go by
Procrastination is a waste of time, like an incarceration lock
Occupations everywhere deal with time
Waiting for the moments are fine
Months into the years
Hanging around with your peers
Achieving success in life and occupation
Time is monitored throughout the nation
Time is what I make of it

The Mind of Another
Rene Manuel Sánchez Sr., Elk River

Where am I, this place so dark and alone? Where have I gone? I see not my way. I look but cannot see. I hear but do not listen. I touch but I cannot feel. Where am I, this place so dark and alone? I then realize; I am in the mind of another.

I speak, but my words are never heard; my footsteps follow me asunder. This word I constantly hear, with such ease, such comfort, again and again. I hear this word always so near. Why does this mind accept such a thing, does it not know this word, this ugly name, this shame? Does it not realize the fear this word has caused throughout the years? This mind of another: why must it think that no harm is done every time this word is said to one another? Why must it be so, in the mind of another?

As I travel from place to place in search of the light, I find only darkness and anger, fear and loathing. What could have caused such damage, a mind once so full of delight? Could it have possibly been that word that has condemned this poor soul to this life of horror and despair? Gone are the days of schoolboy delights.

"The streets and that word are the only things left," he thinks.

But now my journey is complete. He is now like new, that word is no more, for the "Word" has entered into his heart.

Call it what you will, call it magic or not. I simply call it a miracle; in the mind of another.

Wilma Griebel, Southern Minnesota

WISDOM AND LEARNING

My Dream
Fawsiyo Said, Minneapolis

I come from Somalia in East Africa. When I was a little girl, I was planning to be a doctor. As I grew up my country started a civil war. So we came to America, my family and I. Now I want to make my dream come true. I am going to school every day to learn in ELL classes. I will try to get a GED diploma. After I graduate I would like to go to college. I would start my major to become a children's doctor.

Fawsiyo Said is originally from Somalia.

The Meteor Shower
Sao Moua, Oakdale

The meteor shower day was when people saw flying stars with their naked eyes. The stars were flying and moving everywhere. Also, the stars were shaking too. The stars were very shiny. It was the most beautiful night ever.

People believe that when they see a flying star, they should make a wish. I don't believe that. I don't think that wishes will come true. It is just a waste of time for me.

I couldn't believe my eyes when I saw the flying stars. I couldn't believe that I could see the flying stars with my naked eyes. It was so amazing to me. I was so happy when I saw the flying stars from my porch.

It was the best night and dream. After I watched the meteor shower, I could sleep. I couldn't go to sleep before, because I was excited to see the meteor shower. But, after that I could sleep well.

A meteor shower is when many rocks fly through space. People go outside and look at the stars. People were very excited to see the flying stars. On the day I saw the meteor shower it was very cold, but I enjoyed it a lot. I enjoyed the stars and the cold a lot.

My Work
Vita Hladun, Savage

I work every day because I have four children and a fifth child, this is my husband. I have a lot of work during the day. I wake up my children for school. I make my children brush their teeth. I cook food every day and put the plates on the table. I wash dishes and put my youngest son to sleep after lunch. I play with my youngest son when the others sons are in school. I iron once a week. I help the children do their homework every day. I read books to my children every night. I feel tired because I don't have a mother or grandmother or sister to help me with my children. My husband works hard every day. He comes back home, when the children go to bed. I like working for my family. I like spending time with my children, working outside, and shoveling snow. I like picking up toys with my children at night. My work for my family is important to me.

Vita Hladun is originally from Ukraine.

What I Want
Gustav K. Shackelton, Chisholm

What I want is to stay free, far from the penitentiary.
Not smoking weed, trying to achieve my dreams,
Doing it one day at a time.
Trying to find mine
Inner strength, energy pulled straight out of me.
Heading down a wrong road,
Feeling so cold; feeling strange.
Living life on the Range
Wishing my life could change.
Feeling deranged; in and out of a cage.
Stuck in misery; nobody hearing me,
Fearing me, killing me, beating me, teasing me.
Twelve felonies; cops my enemies
Watching me bleed, fearing me because
Resentment and hate; all these drunk nights,
Cold cells, playing their games, paying their wages,
And I'm the one to blame.
But I guess you never learn if you never try.
If you never live, then you really never die.
If you never die, then you never rise up through the sky
Meeting the One who gave His only begotten Son
So whoever believes in Him gets to live in eternity.
So I'm going to get what I want and what I need,
And that is to be free.

Manuel
Manuel Mendoza, Minneapolis

M – My name is Manuel. I like
A – American cheese. My
N – New car is red.
U – Up, the movie, is funny. I am studying
E – English. My
L – Level is beginning

Manuel Mendoza is originally from Mexico.

I am Suzy
Suzy Guerra, Oakdale

Suzy
I am free
Daughter of Margarita
Who needs love
Who loves her children
Who sees the world
Who hates men
Who fears death
Who dreams of flying
Who has found poems of sadness
Resident of judgment
Guerra

Virginia
Virginia García Jiménez, Minneapolis

Virginia
Smart, funny, shy
Who likes music, children, class
Who is afraid of bees, snakes
Who needs books, friends, money
Mother, music, sister

Virginia García Jiménez is originally from Mexico.

My Quiet Place
Bahtiraj Tahir, Elk River

My quiet place is on a basketball court. I chose the court because when I'm alone, I can meditate. I can have my own time and just think things through. I like to shoot baskets alone. It keeps me calm, and all my worries are gone. The air is just perfect, the wind is at the right level, and the sun is not too hot.

At times when I'm alone on the court, the wind hits my face at the right time and the sun is just warm. I can also hear the birds chirping, but my mind is wondering about my problems, my past, and my future. I go to my quiet place also when I'm mad or sad. It helps me calm down or just get right with people. It also helps me get right with God. I think of my sins, and ask God for forgiveness.

Twenty-four Things to Always Remember...and One Thing to Never Forget!
Eang Say, Saint Louis Park

Your presence is a present to the world.
You're unique and one of a kind.
Your life can be what you want it to be.
Take the day just one at a time.
Count your blessings, not your troubles.
You'll make it through whatever comes along.
Within you are so many answers.
Understand, have courage, be strong.
Don't put limits on yourself.
So many dreams are waiting to be realized.
Decisions are too important to leave to chance.
Reach for your peak, your goal, your prize.
Nothing wastes energy more than worrying.
The longer one carries a problem,
The heavier it gets.
Don't take things too seriously.
Live a life of serenity, not a life of regrets.
Remember that a little love goes a long way.
Remember that a lot...goes forever.
Remember that friendship is a wise investment.
Life's treasures are people...together.
Realize that it's never too late.
Do ordinary things in an extraordinary way.
Have health and hope and happiness.
Take the time to wish upon a star.
And don't ever forget...
For even a day...how very
Special you are.

Eang Say is 29 years old and is originally from Siem Reap, Cambodia.

The Homemaker
Pa Houa Thao, Minneapolis

I want to write about my housewife job. I work at home. I started this job in 1995. I work every day. I begin to work at 4:00 a.m. and work to 9:00 p.m. I work Monday to Sunday—seven days a week. I started this job because I love my family. I got married. I know what job I want to do. I will have many children in the future.

My duties in Thailand: I sewed Hmong Pandaos, cooked, washed the dishes, washed clothes, cleaned the house and took care of children. Sometimes it was difficult for me when I had children who were sick.

Another Chance at Life
Lonnie Eubanks, Saint Paul

I am thankful for being free of drugs and alcohol. That is one miserable life to live. I will never go back to that life again. Since I have been drug free for 17 years, I have accomplished many goals that I thought I never could achieve. I own my house, and I am married and have two children. The Harmony Learning Center ABE program has helped me achieve my goals. The teachers are outstanding and also the volunteers. This program has made a big difference in my life. I know if I stick with this program, it will open up many doors for me.

Coming to School
Barb Smead, Saint Paul

One thing I enjoyed in 2009 was waking up and going to school at Harmony. It gives older people things to look forward to. We are not forgotten. This school could bring to life a new author or writer. Young and old can learn at the same level. I am happy to have found Harmony Learning Center.

Thank You
Shukri Ali, Rochester

Thank you all Hawthorne teachers and volunteers. You help us in many ways. We don't come here only for learning. We also come here with all of our problems. You listen to our problems and help us as much as you can. You help us to arrange work training, doctor appointments, and whatever else needs to be resolved that we can't manage on our own. You give us not only the education we need, but also you show us how people can work together to make a difference. We can't thank you enough.

Shukri Ali is originally from Mogadishow, Somalia.

Learning English with My Children
Gadeise Gebywe, Saint Paul

I came to America on February 4, 2004. The first few months here were the hardest. The only things I knew how to say in English were "Yes" and "No." I decided to change my life and the lives of my children, so I started going to school. Every day, one of my kids would offer to help me with my homework. They got me used to the computer and reading books. They gave me 15 words a week and tested me on Friday. I love my kids for helping me and getting me to go to school and change my life in America. I'm the first in my family to go to school, and I'm proud of myself for this. Thanks to my kids and all my teachers. My English is getting better every day, so my life is getting easier in America.

Gadeise Gebywe is 44 years old and is originally from Ethiopia.

I Am Lucky
Victor R. Rosas, Minneapolis

I am lucky because I have health. During my first winter in Minneapolis, I didn't get a cold. Usually, I never have to go to the hospital, because I don't get sick. My friends tell me, "You are a robot, because we never see you sick." Only I go to the hospital when I have to bring a sick friend. Anyway, I eat a lot of fruits and vegetables. That's why I have a healthy body or lucky health.

My Dream
Marcia, Minneapolis

When I was a child I dreamed to be a doctor, but I didn't think it would happen because my parents didn't have enough money to pay for college. I started working when I was 13 years old. I worked in the morning and at night I went to college. While I was studying, my husband was sad because he was going to get a Visa to move to the United States. He wanted to know if I wanted to come with him, but I couldn't get a Visa. I had to find another way to get to the United States. I arrived in this country with a lot of debts in my own country to pay. I had to work very hard when I first came to repay those debts. After I had my daughter I thought about going back to school, but this time for language and then to get my GED. After, I would go to college to get a degree in nursing. But, my dream isn't finished yet. My daughter told me she will become a doctor because she likes to help people as well. So my dream will live in my daughter.

Marcia is originally from Ecuador.

Decision to Pursue My Dream
Lourdes Mendoza, Minneapolis

When I came to the United States, I was single and young. I found two jobs, and both were full time. But I did not realize about education or a better life in the future. I dedicated my life only to working hard. Now, eight years later, my life has changed. I'm still happy, but it's more complicated, because I got married and I have a kid. I thought, "I have to be the example for my family; I want them to feel proud of me."

I decided going to school would be a great idea but there was a problem. How will I take care of my work, family and school? But somebody advised me. He told me, "You just find the time to do what you have to do. Don't worry about how long you leave your family alone, just about the quality of time you are giving to them."

He continued telling me, "Just imagine how your life will change if you get prepared for the future, studying something, getting a career, making more money with less effort, spending time with your family, etc." He inspired me to keep on track.

My dream ever since has always been to have a foundation for kids. I understand anyone who has no family or who lost their parents because I have had the same experiences. Now I want my dreams to come true: studying, working and finding the balance with my family too.

Lourdes Mendoza is 29 years old and is originally from Cuenca, Ecuador.

Money Is the Ruler of All Evil
Kendall Williams, Minneapolis

Money is the thing we all need to live and survive. But money can also be controlling and bring us power and respect. Money is also called cash. Money has a lot of dead presidents on the front of them and "In God We Trust" on the back. Money can influence you to do stupid things—especially when you're broke—like rob banks, steal from other people and break up friendships and family relationships. I feel money has a lot to do with greed. Loving money is not a hard thing to do. That's why we keep in mind, "In God We Trust" so we won't lose focus on each other about money.

My Dream
J. R. Boswell, Minneapolis

I will work very hard to make my dream come true, because if you don't work towards your dream it will never come true. Sometimes I sit down and think about my reading and writing. I know I have to work on it to make my dream come true, because my dream is to get a GED and go to college. My dream will affect my family because I will be able to get a better job to take care of them. I know my dream will come true because when you work hard nothing is impossible in the U.S.

If I don't work hard on it that dream will never come true for me. Sometimes it takes time to come true. Without my mother I would never have a dream. It is very important to everyone to be happy and to see their dream come true and have the job of their life. My mother has 16 children and I am the only one in the United States. In my country life is hard, but I want to work hard to make a life better for my family and me. I will do what it takes to make my brother and sister happy. I said to my father before he passed away, "Dad, I will be the son and work hard and make the rest of the family happy and do what is best for you and mom in Jamaica." I still plan to do this.

J. R. Boswell is 29 years old and is originally from Jamaica.

Experiment
Daniel García, Minneapolis

This story is about a group of scientists who did an experiment. I don't know if this story was real or fake. I don't even remember if I saw it in a movie or somebody told me about it. Well, the scientist had a little dog in a cage living in regular conditions fitting her. They were good and clean. Everything was OK, but after a couple months, they electrified one wall of the cage. At first, she took the electricity discharge, and she realized quickly that she had to stay away from that wall of the cage. After awhile, they added electricity to other walls. Then, she learned that she couldn't touch those two walls of the cage. After another while, they added electricity to the other two walls, and the little dog had no way to move except through the floor. She carefully tried not to touch any of the walls, because they were dangerous. But the mad scientist added electricity also to the floor. Oh boy!! The little dog went crazy. She was trying to escape while jumping and screaming. She had no place to stay or stand without receiving those electrical charges. But after awhile, she stopped fighting, and she was just waiting for the electricity without complaint—just laying down waiting for the charges. At the end, the scientists thought that that experiment was done, so they wanted to treat that poor little dog, but something weird happened. When they opened the door of the cage to let her go, she didn't go anywhere. That cage was her home. She wanted to stay inside. The little dog had been accustomed to those situations. Those things were part of her life.

As I told you, I don't know if this is truth or not, but I think that the same things happen to some of us. We are used to living with many problems—really bad situations—and holding onto them for years. I mean we need to open our eyes and take care of ourselves more. If we can't leave the problems, please be brave and look or ask for help.

The Town
Miguel Angel Bautista, Saint Paul

I grew up in a little town called Hidalgo, Mexico, where everyone knew each other.

I come from a poor farmer's family. At an early age, I started to work and help my parents. In the morning I was in school and the afternoon I was a shepherd and farmer. I was still a child and small, so I couldn't do everything, but I did everything I could do.

I have always dreamed of going to college, but when you don't have enough money to pay for it, there are two choices: stay there in my town or migrate to a different place. That's why I am here, trying to reach the American Dream.

I have been here for almost five years, working so hard every day. During the day

I am going to work, and at night I come to school to learn English. I have been working in construction since I arrived in the United States. Now I have my own business, so I can say that I am reaching some of my goals. It has been difficult to have the things that I have. But I am grateful too, because now I can do many things that I couldn't do before I came here.

Miguel Angel Bautista is 22 years old and is originally from Mexico.

Dream
Isabel, Minneapolis

I am going to try to close my eyes and look into my heart to find a little girl dressed in a green uniform. She is in the tenth grade of high school. She is very happy, because she got an excellent score.

One morning, the teacher of literature asked her, "What are you going to be in your future?" The happy girl answered, "I'm going to be a teacher like you." The girl worked so hard and got a certificate. She was very proud of herself. Then, she made an application for a teacher's position, but she had just an excellent certificate, not money or political influence. So, she was disappointed and had to understand that in many societies there are bad situations. One of them is corruption.

I am from Ecuador, and I'm trying to have my dream come true. Any help is very welcome!

Hope, Dreams and Future
Janette Rojas, Minneapolis

My hope is to finish my CDA course. In this course, I am learning how to teach, take care of children, and work with them. I decided to be a teacher, because I enjoy watching children grow up. After I finish my CDA, I want to go to Minneapolis Technical Community College. I want to get 35 credits to be a lead teacher. One of my dreams is to work in a Hispanic Daycare where I can help children whose English is not their first language. I also want to keep my culture and traditions with my children. Some children who were born in the United States lose their culture and their own language. I don't want my own people to lose our culture. That's why I want to teach and keep my language and traditions with my children.

In the future, I hope all my dreams will come true and my own people will think that it is true that this is not our country. We have to learn English and the American culture, but we haven't forgotten that we're Latin, and Spanish is our first language.

> In Somalia, parents pay the cost of their children's education from elementary school on.

Differences in Education
Saeed Abdulle, Minneapolis

In both Somalia and the U.S. education is very important, but there are a lot of different rules in each country. First, in the United States, school is free, from elementary school to high school. In Somalia, school is not free at all. In Somalia parents pay the cost of their children's education from elementary school on.

In Somalia, boys and girls are separated; there are schools for boys and schools for girls. The only time boys and girls are in the same school is when they are in elementary school. In the United States, boys and girls are in the same schools and classes.

Another difference is that Somali schools have uniforms. There are specific uniforms for elementary school, middle school and high school. But in the United States most schools don't have uniforms.

Also in Somalia, students call their teacher "Teacher." They do not call him or her by name. In the United States, students use their teacher's name.

In Somalia, there is no breakfast or lunch for students. Some students bring their own lunch from home or they buy it at school. But in the United States, there is breakfast and lunch available for each student at school, every day.

These are some of the educational differences between Somalia and the United States.

My Journey with a Disability
Zalina Khan, Brooklyn Park

I moved to the United States when I was 30. I moved here from Guyana, South America. In Guyana, there are no programs for people with disabilities, and they do not have the opportunity to go to school. When I was 12, my dad began to teach me at home. He continued helping me develop skills until I was 21. It is difficult for me to communicate verbally, making it hard to ask questions while learning. After moving to the United States, for the first time I got the chance to work a real job and go to a real school. For the first time in my life, I had a voice. I was introduced to a communication device, finally allowing me to have conversations with others. Now, I also have programs which help me with school, work and living as independently as possible. In the future, I want to graduate and go to college. In college, I want to study child development. Eventually, I would love to work with children and run my own daycare. I would also love to get married and have children of my own. I really enjoy school and all of my teachers.

Zalina Khan is originally from Guyana, South America.

Education
Asha Mohamed, Minneapolis

My name is Asha Mohamed, and I am from Somalia. In my country, the education has not been important to our people for the last 20 years because of civil war. Twenty years ago, our country was one of the best countries in Africa and education was the number one concern for our people. Life was quiet and beautiful. But our people were suddenly fighting for no reason. They made the country a mess. Everything broke down and life became miserable. People no longer thought about education. The number one goal of the Somali people became the survival of themselves and their children.

In the U.S., most of us go to school, and we try to recover from that lack of education. Most of the first people who arrived in the U.S. in 1998 and before, finished their education. Today, they have their own lives. But since 2001, Somali education in the U.S.

Dan Selberg, Brooklyn Park

has gotten worse, especially for the boys. They forget the reason they are here in the U.S. They forget the big chance they have here in America that those in Somalia do not. They forget their poor mothers who have tried to let them become the best they can be. They forget the beautiful country of Somalia that is waiting for them to come back one day. The Somali youth of the U.S. are the only chance our country has. This is a problem we have in the U.S.

Education
Ahmed Firin, Minneapolis

My name is Ahmed Firin. I fled my country in 1990 when the Civil War broke out. I fled with all my family members to Ethiopia, which is a neighboring country of Somalia. We left our home and all our property was looted. We came to Ethiopia without money and joined the refugee camp. After spending several years suffering in the refugee camp we got started in the resettlement process from the U.S. government. Our life in the refugee camp was really very horrible, so I did not go to high school.

Do you know how important education is? It is very hard to survive without education, so brothers and sisters, I encourage you to learn as much knowledge as you can.

When I came to the United States I did not know English. I did not know how to speak, read or write, so daily life was difficult. I did not understand people or the foreign culture. Every country has its own unwritten culture, so I decided to attempt to learn how to understand people.

I started hard work in a factory. I usually went to work early in the evening. When I got home I took off my shoes and changed my clothes. I was very tired, so I could not go to school. I just ate dinner and went to bed.

I encourage all my friends to continue their education and don't give up because education is very important.

FAQs to Me in the USA
Ilavarasi Selvam, Plymouth

Hello Friends. My name is Ilavarasi, I am from India. I came to the USA in 2007. I didn't know about the ESL class till July 2009. Before the ESL class my English was not very good, I was not fluent enough and I needed to practice the accent here. Once I knew about this class, I met many people of different cultures from different countries. And also through volunteering at school and libraries I was able to practice my speech. And from all the people I met there and at my class, I heard the same two questions repeatedly. Why are Indians good in speaking English? My answer to them was yes, because India was ruled by the British for nearly 200 years (from 1751 to 1947), and so their influence helped us in speaking the language fluently.

Second question, they all asked me was when Indians meet in class or somewhere else, why do we communicate or talk in English? Chinese, Koreans, Russians, Somalians and other cultures choose to communicate or talk in their mother language.

For this I explained that India is a country with 28 different states and each state has its

> Every country has its own unwritten culture, so I decided to attempt to learn how to understand people.

own language, so we all can understand each other by communicating in English, the one language that is common among us. These questions made me wonder, because before I didn't acknowledge how many languages my country has. Since so many people asked me about it why not write a Journal Entry on this? Let everyone know how many languages India has. That is why I wrote my journal on these questions. Thank you for all who read this Journal.

Ilavarasi Selvam is 36 years old and is originally from India.

My English Education
Siriporn, Rochester

In November 2008, I moved to Rochester, Minnesota for work. A few weeks after I arrived, I settled down in my new apartment. I began living in American society. However, I didn't understand what most people were talking about. People often used slang and idioms to express and emphasize what they were saying. For example, "buck" was a slang term for a dollar; likewise, "pig" meant police. What did it feel like if "I was on cloud nine," or something "knocked my socks off?" Moreover, people spoke very fast and all words blended together. In addition, some same words could have different meanings depending on the speaker's usage and intonation. The way people spoke wasn't what I had learned from my English class. The first thing that came to my mind at the time was what it was like to have everyone around you speak an alien language.

I started studying English in elementary school. All the books were British English and focused on vocabulary and grammar. Students had to memorize a lot of words and grammar rules. This memorization was very boring for many students. In my opinion, studying English wasn't fun, and we didn't speak English very often in Thailand. As a result, I didn't pay attention in English class, because I didn't think English was important.

At the university level, I had to read many English text books. Even though all the books were written in English, I primarily focused on technical terms and math equations. After I graduated, I used limited English writing at work and spread sheets, charts or diagrams in most of my communication with co-workers. I barely used English outside of work.

However, I now live in the USA, and I have many difficulties at work and outside of work.

I can't communicate to other people. I don't enjoy watching TV or listening to music like I had in Thailand. I have begun a project to improve my English skill and seek an English school in Rochester. Hawthorne Education Center is that school and provides many English classes for the community. I have attended conversation and writing classes for one year. Moreover, I continue to study vocabulary, listen to music, watch TV and speak English with other people every day. Although I feel like I am swallowing bitter medicine, it is the only way to make a happy life in the USA.

Siriporn is originally from Thailand.

Tennis Life
Oleg, Minneapolis

A lot of people in the world prefer sports activities. Sports exercise helps people keep their bodies and brains in good mental and physical condition as long as possible for their whole life. As for me, tennis is the best sport in my life.

I started to play tennis when I was 22 years old. Before I started, I'd seen that very interesting game on TV and have loved it for all my life. I spent many hours learning the rules and practicing, practicing, practicing before I could do the activities right and feel the racket and keep my vision on the ball. Step-by-step, I discovered new opportunities in that game and in myself. Even if I didn't practice so much, I wasn't nervous and started to do it again.

Tennis has stayed as part of my life. After a couple years of practice, I started to play in competition in very different tournaments. Also, I have met new friends and interesting people in my life, and I have good relationships.

Tennis has made me stronger and my brain smarter. For those reasons, I recommend that all people play tennis and have more enjoyment and fun in life through the sport.

My Story
AP, Minneapolis

Hi my name is Alex and I'm from Cuenca, Ecuador, South America. I'm going tell this history of how I started to work in this company. First thing, I have been living in Minnesota for five years. I have my sisters and brothers here, but my parents still live there in my town. I miss them so much, but I hope someday to go back and be together with them.

Since 2004, I started to work in a greenhouse. This job is about growing plants (flowers). It is one of my favorite jobs. In the summer, it's a little hot, but it is OK because it is a busy time. I don't feel too hot. I move full carts of the plants. Sometimes I help my wonderful customers. At Christmas time, it is so good! We sell Christmas trees and I have a lot of fun doing that. I like the people who work with me, because we are a good team. Like everyone, I have a future dream in life. I like to drive. The first thing I would like to do is have my commercial driver's license. I want to be a truck driver and I thank whoever reads my history.

AP is 26 years old and is originally from Cuenca, Ecuador.

My Past and My Future
Melese Abebe, Apple Valley

I was born in Ethiopia in 1984. I finished high school in 2002. After I graduated from high school, my dream was to go to university and study electrical engineering. To do that, I should study very hard. Six weeks later, I joined Mekele University, but I couldn't get in the electrical engineering department. Instead of that, I got in the chemistry department. I wasn't happy learning chemistry for six weeks. After six weeks, I loved the chemistry department. I scored excellent results in chemistry. I studied chemistry for four years. I finished my Bachelor's degree in chemistry in 2006. After I graduated, I taught chemistry for three years until August 20, 2009.

I came to the United States on September 19, 2009. Now I have two plans. My first plan is to go to university here and study pharmacy. My second plan is to help my poor relatives. Finally I will marry and I will have three kids.

Melese Abebe is 26 years old and is originally from Ethiopia.

Writer's Itch
Anonymous, Duluth

Boozhoo (Hello),
I am a 71-year-old American Native Ojibwe Elder, adding yet another chapter in my life. I volunteer for the Disaster Relief Project, rebuilding and providing homes for the victims of Hurricane Katrina. I am a handywoman,

capable of doing a man's job, such as carpentry, sheetrock, laying floors. Four years after Katrina, the environmental destruction and polluted water still lingers.

Working at the project's sites, I could not find the words to describe my feelings or experiences, to write the history, the destruction seen by the survivors and witnesses. I was ashamed I could not write.

The years of staring at blank pages and remaining speechless led to frustration and lack of confidence. For the first time in years, I re-examined my reading and writing skills. I enrolled in Adult Learning Center classes. The instructors gave me suggestions, reading materials, 1:1 mentoring, and encouragement. Rethinking and shaping sentences was not easy. I have written two business letters, a letter to the newspaper editor, personal letters and, finally, the Disaster Relief Journal.

The excellent teaching staff at the Adult Learning Center has given me hope. I have gained the confidence I needed to express myself and the ability to write and develop sentences.

As a Native Elder, I have a vision to be a woman of letters, journals, a creative writer of children's books, to be a storyteller of Native cultures for the tribe. I want to let the words flow from my hands and end with writer's cramps.

Miigwech (Thank You)
Mindimouyenh (Old Lady)

The Importance of Education
Anonymous, Eagan

I am sure if you want to be successful in your future life, you need to have a good education. As an adult, making a good decision about what you want to study is hard—especially if you are looking for something you like to do and want to feel excited about a job you do day after day.

Getting a good education is not easy or cheap so you need determination, commitment, and very hard work to achieve it. However, every effort you do to get a good education is worth it, because your future and your family's future will be impacted in many ways.

My goal as an ABE student is to achieve some training so I can get a good paying job that I enjoy doing. Getting a good paying job will help me to have extra money to travel with my family, help my family back in Mexico, and pay for my children's university. That is my dream.

My teacher, Laurie, is helping me to reach my goals. She does everything she can to help me. I'm so glad this program exists, because not only am I learning English, studying for the GED, and gaining parenting skills, but my kids are getting a good education in the family schoolroom as well.

I think without this program many of us will have no chance at all to learn English. Everything this program offers is great and the way the teachers and staff work with us is amazing. I hope they all know they are helping us to change our lives.

The Best Changes in Technology
Wesley Fontes, Owatonna

The first and most important change that affected us, including me, is wireless technologies; this solved many problems that we had. These technologies came to us through cell phones, access to the Internet, Global Position System (GPS), Worldwide Interoperability for Microwave Access (WiMax) and other devices that we use to communicate, all these without physical access.

Other changes are the development of the Internet, the creation of many search and social networking websites, which can provide to us several facilities that help us every day.

The technologies that really have potential and are developing are the unification of the protocols that will connect all electronic devices, so that one can communicate or control the other. So you are in bed, and want to do something that needs to wake you up, if you have a laptop with this kind of technology, you can use it to turn on or off all electronic stuff that you have, and also you can use your cell phone to control your laptop or things like that.

Wesley Fontes is 21 years old and is originally from Brazil.

Juan Valdez
Sandra McGraw, Saint Paul

Colombia is my home land. I want to explain who Juan Valdez is. He represents coffee growers in Colombia. He symbolizes more than 560,000 Colombian coffee farmers. He always appears with his donkey named "Conchita," carrying sacks of harvested coffee beans. In addition, he always advertised Colombian coffee on TV, radio, and sometimes in international movies. He has traveled all over the world promoting this popular product.

Regarding the Juan Valdez character: first, Colombia wants to prove that Colombia has the best soil components, altitude, and a wide variety of coffee. And second, this advertising represents a huge association of coffee growers.

In conclusion, if you want to get to know this symbol, you should check out either on the bottom of a coffee bag or can. Otherwise, if you decide to buy it, it means you are drinking the best quality of Colombian coffee and supporting many Colombian families to improve their life. Do not be surprised if you sometimes see Juan Valdez and his donkey, Conchita, walking around aisles of your local supermarket.

Sandra McGraw is originally from Columbia.

How Do You Think TV Affects Your Family?
Claudia Quevedo, Shakopee

I think TV is good because we watch news for information, what is happening in other states. But sometimes some people like to watch TV all day. They watch TV all day sitting in the living room. They need to exercise and that affects the person. Some like to watch TV programs that have action and terror, for example today I watched TV in the morning about an earthquake. In Haiti when children watch TV all day it is not good because children do not learn in school when they watch TV programs, and many movies. Soap operas have many sex scenes. I think that it is not good for children; when children watch violent TV programs they behave badly. They think TV is real but only the news is real, because the other programs are fiction. I think TV affects my family, because when

Joni G Sperandio, Maple Lake

we go to sleep or school we think about the program that we watched and we do not concentrate. We have to sleep and think that what happened the other day can affect everybody.

Global Warming in Hong Kong
Ho Chee Lau, Cloquet

I can feel the global warming here in Hong Kong. There were four seasons in Hong Kong when I was small. Now there are just two seasons here, they are summer and winter. It should be a long summer and a short winter exactly. The hurricanes are forceful and more powerful every year. Although, they don't cause any damage to buildings in Hong Kong because they are built for them. In winter, the monsoons that come from northern China become less powerful than before. In short, we get a long hot humid summer and a short humid winter. The short winter will soon be gone in the near future. Hong Kong will then become a tropical area.

Ho Chee Lau is originally from Hong Kong.

Memories
Deka Farah, Minneapolis

I remember when I was in eigth grade. I used to hate math because one of my teachers made me hate it, but I was good at history. My math teacher was strange. All the students hated him because every time he came to class without teaching anything, he said that you are all grounded. After the punishment, he gave us a lot of homework which was 80 questions and said that we should finish them by tomorrow.

Next week he did it again. Then the students were very upset, so they made a plan, and they waited for him outside. Then they got into a fight with him.

Every time I had math class, I used to hate it because all he gave us was a lot of homework and nothing else. Each one of the students complained about him. However, he was a very strange teacher. Actually, he was the worst teacher I have ever seen. Finally, the principal noticed him and he transferred him somewhere else. Thank God!

Walk on the Beach
Anita Radnuz, Saint Paul

When you walk along the ocean, you can see conch shells on the shore. If you put the shell up to your ear, you can hear the ocean sound. The sound of waves moves back and forth. The sound is so beautiful to the ear and mind. You can imagine seeing the ocean in your mind. When I was a kid, I had a friend who gave me a conch shell. I would hold the shell and dream that I was at the ocean.

Child Welfare
Kamella Wahidi, Blaine

This article is about how much money is spent for child welfare in industrialized countries. If I had $140,000 to spend on one child, I would spend it on food and clothes. If I had more money, I would spend it on education and healthcare. I think a safe place to live is very important for children. I would like to spend more money on younger children, because they need to be happy and healthy. It's a good start for life. If I had more money, for the older children I would like to give them a part-time job in my house and back yard. I would make sure they stayed in school and got a good education and they become smart students and cool kids. Maybe I would love them like my own kids.

My Favorite Job

Nursing is my favorite job. I was a nurse before I came to the USA. I think I still want to be a nurse in the USA.

When I was a kid, my health was not good. I went to the hospital many times every month. At that time, I didn't like hospitals. So, every time when I went to the hospital I always cried. But one good thing I got from the hospital is that it made me feel better. I always remember the nurses' smiles. When I cried, the nurses always came to me, smiled at me, talked nicely and read stories. So at that time, I thought I liked nurses, but not hospitals.

After I grew up, when I went to the hospital, I always saw that nurses smiled at patients, made them feel better and gave them hope. I thought that was the most beautiful smile in the world. I wanted to be a nurse when I grew up. I wanted to give this smile to people, give them happiness and hope. I wanted every one to remember "The Nurse Smile."

Junjie Huang is an ESL student in Saint Michael – Albertville Community Education Center. She came from China. After graduation from nursing school, she worked for a hospital in her home town before she came to the USA. She is 31 years old. She is a mom now with a 7-year-old boy and a 3-year-old girl. She likes reading books, enjoying music and playing with her kids. She lives in Saint Michael and is taking classes at Saint Cloud State University.

Doing Medical Assembly

I am a refugee from Liberia to the Ivory Coast and Ghana for resettlement. I came on September 14th, 2005. I started school to improve my life. I got a job on December 2nd, 2005, doing medical assembly for hearing aids. At my job, I work faster. The computer is programmed to make one part in 19 seconds, but I can make one in 16 seconds. The inspector calls me a witch because I am so fast.

Zack Anderson is a student in the Metro North ABE Program, Blaine Learning Lab. Zack came to the United States almost five years ago from Liberia as a refugee through Ghana. Zack now lives in Brooklyn Park and works at InTec Industry. Zack wants to be an auto mechanic after going to college.

My First Words in English
Anonymous, Saint Paul

I don't remember which English word was the first one that I learned, but I remember how I felt about not speaking English. Not understanding the people made me feel deaf, mute, stupid, and angry, like when you go to the doctor, if you don't speak English, you must have an interpreter. I would always ask myself, "Why do I have to tell this lady what is wrong with me? She is not even a doctor!"

So I remember one day after going to the doctor, I went to the store, and they were selling a book called "Inglés En Español." What they meant was that they spell the word in English and spell the pronunciation in Spanish. So I bought it, and read it over and over. It was funny, but every time that I've learned a new word, I started to hear it often.

At first, I just felt comfortable saying, "Hi, how are you?" "What's your name?" "What time is it?" "It is 'whatever' time." I just knew the words, but to be honest, I never used them. I was afraid to start up a conversation. I remember the first time that I talked in English, I was in a park and a teenager approached me and said, "Excuse me, what time is it?" And I answered, "It is 4 o'clock." And she said, "Mom, it is 4 o'clock." And I was so happy because she understood me.

So I started asking people who knew English, "How should I say this or that?" I remember I used to stare at people's lips, because I wanted to make sure that I pronounced the words correctly. I do not know when I started to write in English, but I do know that I still have a lot to learn.

> And I was so happy because she understood me.

My Dream
Nereo, Minneapolis

I hope in the future all the people who are in an emergency will receive medical attention at hospitals without anyone caring about social status. I hope too, that in the future all people would work without being afraid of not having legal status to work. I believe that the government in this country will accept people based on their work and progress. I think my dream will come true and everyone will have the same opportunities to progress as equals.

Nereo is 26 years old and is originally from Mexico.

My Mother is Proud of My Education
Anonymous, Saint Paul

My mother always said to me, "You have to go to school, because when we were in Africa I didn't go to school." My mother said I could not have free education in Africa. In Africa, it is not easy to get an education. It is very hard to find what makes you happy. When you want to learn English and other subjects, you have to pay money, but here, it is not like that. Everything's paid for by the government. My mother gave me advice, saying not to lose your opportunities. She told my older brother, who is in college in Saint Paul, that knowledge is the light of our lives and it makes us know how to understand people. It also shows us how to communicate, to give our opinions and ideas, and to share the things we learn. That is the advice from my dear mother that I think about all of the time. She told us that someday we would remember what she had said. I am very touched by how much my dear mother loves me. I love her so deeply too.

I Am Lucky
Angel Cruz, Minneapolis

I feel lucky since I moved to Minneapolis. I feel lucky because I have a job. I moved here in May 2001 and I have been working without a problem. I feel lucky because all my co-workers are nice and friendly. I know what I do for work is just to clean offices, but at least I have a job. I feel lucky because I know so many nice people who are around me. I feel lucky because I have family here too, and I don't feel lonely. I feel lucky because I am taking English class at Lehmann Center and all teachers are great and nice to me. That is why I feel lucky.

English Classes
Miao Zhen, Apple Valley

I come from China. I have two children. I have been in America since 2005. I can speak a little English. I can't understand every word. So when my children went to school, I started ESL classes. I want to learn more English to help my children with their homework.

To Be Human
Alvaro Cruz, Minneapolis

It is very interesting to be part of the population in this world. I can't imagine how many people live in this world. There exist a lot of mysteries about humans. We are all considered humans, I think, because all the people are the same physically. Of course, everybody has different feelings, thoughts or just different ways of being.

I really like to talk with all of the people that are interested in knowing more about ourselves. I'm sure that most people don't know why or how we got here, obviously, including me. That would be something very interesting and important to know.

On the other hand, I would like to know or study why people act in different ways. Well, I like to listen and pay attention when somebody talks. That is very important for me because everybody always has something different to say or to do.

We are considered the smartest kind of life in this world compared to other ones, but I don't know if all the people are sure of this. I can't imagine how beautiful and interesting it would be if we all had very good thinking.

As we know, everybody has the right to think or do whatever they want. I would like to tell all of the people that for the first time in their lives, think a little bit about what exactly we are doing here and from where we came.

Finally, I hope some day to understand and that other people will understand, too. Being humans is a big mystery—a mystery that can maybe never be discovered. Also, I'd like to let people know that this mystery some day can be resolved.

My Life
Begeh, Minneapolis

I was born in a small West African country called Senegal, a neighboring country to my parents' native homeland. When I was a little girl, we moved back to their homeland. I had a wonderful life as a child. There was no doubt about that. I was almost always happy and also very close to my parents. They were so much fun to be with and very industrious.

As I grew up, I began to realize that there was something missing in my life and that was the ability to read and write. So, I started to study with some of my friends who were attending school at the time. We studied together for awhile. Then one day, I asked my parents if I could go to school.

They reminded me that I was the one that chose not to go to school, so that is why they let me be. I said I wish you would've encouraged me more, and they said well, you can try again. This time it was the school that said there was no class for children aged 11 to 12 to start grade one. So that was the end of that.

I continued my studies until I was age 16. I enrolled in adult school where they taught skills that were sewing-related and some English. After two years of school, I graduated with a diploma at the end.

I was proud, but it was just the beginning. I continued to search for education. I attended a typing school for three months and then got a visa to join my husband in the United States of America. This was the second time for us to be together in four years. We have been living in Minnesota for eleven years now. We have four wonderful children. They mean the world to me. That makes my life seem complete, but I don't think so. Because after all the fun and happy times, I am still pursuing my education.

Begeh is originally from Senegal.

Not Too Late to Learn
Chavelle Jackson, Minneapolis

My name is Chavelle Jackson. I am a GED student at the age of 28, soon to be 29. I am a GED student because I decided to drop out of high school when I was done with the tenth grade. I grew up in Chicago, Illinois in the ghetto surrounded by drugs and violence. When I was growing up, I went to school and played lots of sports. I also had lots of friends and family, some good and some not.

I dropped out of high school at the age of 16 and chose the wrong path in life. When I was 17, I had my first kid and then later I had several more. I stayed away from books and school for almost 12 years, so I thought it was too late for me to go back to school and get an education. After seeing my kids grow up and hearing words of encouragement from loved ones, I decided to give it a try. It took a lot of guts, but I did it and it's great. I couldn't be any happier with myself right now; even my kids are proud of me for going back to school. When I finish school for my GED, I plan to further my education by taking up a trade and some college.

It feels good to finally get back to school. It makes me feel important and makes me feel like I can do something with myself and for my kids. I think it's very important to have an education, because it opens up many more doors for success and opportunity. I love school, and I am going to keep moving forward with my education.

> It took a lot of guts, but I did it and it was great. I couldn't be happier with myself right now; even my kids are proud of me for going back to school.

Untitled
Igor Dadashev, Saint Louis Park

What is the general purpose of human life? What were we born for? Is our life just a long road from birth to death? I have looked for that answer since my young adulthood. I started my searching when I came home from the army. The wisest philosophers and some scientists tried to give me the answer, but I'm not satisfied with their definitions of human life. I asked some priests and I wasn't satisfied either. Because every religion teaches right things, but unfortunately I see their words are often different or even opposite with their deeds, so is that the truth?

There is a popular Russian proverb about a main goal of man's life. If you want to be a successful person you have to plant a tree, to build your own house, and also grow a son; give him a good education, and you should be a great example for him and other people.

What more can I say? Some people moved to the U.S. because they were poor and unhappy at home. Other ones came here for more possibilities and a good career. When I asked some immigrants about their reasons for immigration, most of them answered me: "It's easy, pal! We looked for a comfortable life, and also a lot of money, a big house and a new car. That's all." It's just a common answer I've heard from everyone.

So what is my goal in life? I have planted more than a singular tree. I built a few houses when I was younger. I have a son and soon I will be a grandfather. But I'm still young and healthy. I can do more than I do now. My searching for the human's life goal is very important for me. I believe in Love and Goodness, but they're not enough in the modern world. I ask myself every day what can I do, what should I do and I can't find an answer. I would be very appreciative if someone could help me. I moved to the U.S. because of my parents. They have lived here since 1996. I love them a lot, and I have my duty for them. That's why I live here in Minnesota. I'm happy to meet good people and improve my English, but I'd like to find the truth and understand the main purpose of my life.

Untitled
Araceli Ramírez, Minneapolis

Araceli is married, I like
Radio every day
Are has two surprises. She
Cooks hot dogs. Her
Eyes are brown. I
Like the food Chinese
Is a good woman.

Araceli Ramírez is originally from Mexico.

Jayson Knutson, Bemidji

Thomas Nelson, Richfield

Friends and Family

From Acapulco to Minnesota
Isabel Sánchez, Apple Valley

I am from Mexico. I have three siblings. My mother worked very hard since I was six years old. I came here twelve years ago. My two sons were born here. Three years ago, my sister told me my father was very sick. We went back to Mexico so my father could know my sons. Five months after that, he died.

My family lived in Acapulco. It is beautiful. I like it so much. I had two uncles there. There were scuba divers. When I went to the beach, they gave me fish and lobster. Fifteen days ago, one uncle died. I miss him.

Isabel Sánchez is originally from Mexico.

My Lovely Remarkable Husband
Faduma Said, Minneapolis

My name is Faduma. My husband and I were born in Somalia. We have been married for six years. We have two cute boys. They are very smart. I would like to talk about my remarkable husband. He is the one who I was looking for in my life. He is the one who always makes me happy. He is my heart. We respect each other. We have a goal to raise our children to have good behavior and to be good role models for them. We wish our life to continue until the end of the world.

Faduma Said is originally from Somalia.

A Scary Memory Before I Was 10 Years Old
Mauricio Cruz, Minneapolis

When I was between 9 and 10 years old, I used to take care of my donkeys after school. I used to take them to pasture and to the water. I had four donkeys: three adult donkeys and one young donkey. I used to use them to carry firewood or other things. It was a weekend in autumn at about 1 p.m. I was riding one of my donkeys. I was taking them to the water. The donkey that I was riding saw another donkey that was near there. It started to run after that donkey. I fell down on the rocks; I scratched my knees and hands. I was so scared. I thanked God that I didn't fracture my head or arms. I got up. I rushed to catch my donkey. When I caught the donkey that ran away, I went to tie it down. The next day, I had sore knees and hands. I told my father about the incident. He told me never to ride the donkey again.

My Sweet Mom
Qalbinur Ahmed, Minneapolis

When I was eight years old, I remembered my mom went to a different state. That time I was a young girl. When I remembered, I started to cry, but my grandma said, "Please don't cry, baby." One day I said, "Grandma, I need my mom, please." After that my

Friends and Family - 89

grandma said, "I will call your mom soon." Two years later, my mom came in the night. I heard some voices and I woke up startled, half asleep. A few minutes later, I looked around my room and saw my mom. I jumped off my bed and gave her the biggest hug ever.

Qalbinur Ahmed is originally from Somalia.

My Childhood Friend
Ngae Lay, Saint Paul

I was a child. I was nine years old. My friend's name was Htway Htway. One day in my school, we had a party and we danced a Karen dance. When we danced the Karen dance, at that time my childhood friend fell down under the stage. The teachers, parents, and students laughed. That time my friend was very embarrassed. I have never forgotten my friend's face, even until right now.

Ngae Lay is originally from Burma.

The Best Day of My Life
María Guaman, Minneapolis

The best day of my life was when my husband asked me, "Do you want to marry me?" I said to him, "Yes," but my mom and my dad didn't like him. They always said, "No, you can't marry him." I asked, "Why?" And they answered "Because he has a lot of girlfriends." But I loved my husband. I thought to myself and I said, "I'm not going to obey my mom now."

I was 20 years old in that time and my husband had 18 years. He said to me, "If your mom and your dad don't let us marry we should go far from here." He said, "Let's go to Quito." Quito is the Capital of Ecuador. We went there for one year. It was a big city. After one year, we returned to the town where my mom lived. When we came back, my mom and my dad said, "We forgive you about it. We are happy now because you came back with us." After that, we got married. Now I live in Minneapolis. I have two kids, Sonia and Tom. They are in the school and we are a happy family, thank God.

María Guaman is originally from Ecuador.

My Grandsons
Junru Tang, Apple Valley

I am from China. I have been in the United States for four years. I live with my daughter's family. In the U.S., I have seen a lot of things different from China. Every day, my two grandsons go to school with a school bus. That is safe for children. When they come back home from school, they have only a little homework. On Halloween day, they wore special clothes and played games. My grandsons also joined the hockey team.

Sometimes we travel to another state. Last year, we went to Fargo, North Dakota. I felt very happy.

Junru Tang is 57 years old and is originally from China.

My Story
Nay Lorbliayao, Minneapolis

In my country, I have eight sisters and four brothers. Much of my family has died. My mother is 80 years old. She is a very old woman. She lives with my father. They live in a little house.

My father is unhappy, because he is older and he is very sick. Sometimes I called my mother. She is happy. She said a lot to me. She asked me, "Do you know your Father is older? You don't want to come to visit him?"

I told my mother, "I need three more years.

I will be over there because now my daughter is too small, and I don't have someone helping me to take care of her, and I have to study now. I believe my father has a long time to live with you. You don't worry about it."

How do I to tell my mom that in my life I don't have money to buy the ticket to visit them? How I haven't helped myself enough yet. Maybe sometimes my mom thought I had a nice life in the United States. I have to forget them now and not think about that, because I don't want to tell them about my life. I don't want them to worry about my life.

However, in my life, I want to tell them I'm okay, you don't have to worry about me like that.

This Is Why I Know We Love Each Other
Mohamed-Deq Warsame, Minneapolis

I remember the place, the date, the time, and the way she looked at me. The beautiful face with the smile, the respect she gave me and how shy she was. It was the first time I met her. From that time, this is what I call love.

Love is when we go out to eat and I give her most of my French fries without making her give me any of hers. Love is what makes me smile when I am tired. Love is when she makes coffee and she takes a sip before giving it to me to make sure the taste is okay. If you want to learn to love better you should start with a friend who you hate.

Love is hugging, love is kissing, and love is saying no. Love is when she tells me that she likes my shirt so I wear it every day. Love is when she gives me the best piece of chicken.

You really shouldn't say "I love you" unless you mean it, but if you mean it you should say it a lot. People forget this. You have to fall in love before you get married. Then when you are married you can sit around and read books together. You can break love, but it won't die. Love cures people, both the ones who give it and the ones who receive it. The hunger for love is much more difficult to remove than the hunger for bread.

Love is when I ask myself a question about her and I get a positive answer in return. Love is when I smile from nothing but memory. I know what love is because of my sweetheart, Nasra.

Mohamed-Deq Warsame is originally from Somalia.

Marami
Johara Hassan, Minneapolis

When I was ten years old, I was so happy all the time because I didn't know anything about life. The only things I cared about were the things that made me happy; for example, playing with children.

We used to play a special game. We called that game "Marami." When we began to play, we made a circle. Then one person ran around the circle with half of a towel. He dropped it behind someone. If that person couldn't see the towel, we called that person "dead." If the person knew the towel was behind him he could run around the circle to the next person. So I used to have fun. I hope it will come again one day.

Johara Hassan is 24 years old and is originally from Ethiopia.

My Baby Boy
Rachel, Red Wing

Having a one year old child has its rewards. Nothing makes me happier than when I can tickle him and he giggles or watch him open and close cupboards. In the past three months, I have watched him walk across the living room. William has brought my sister, my dad and me closer together. It's nice.

There are disadvantages to having a one year old child if you're a single mom. He relies on only me and it's a struggle. Working does not allow me to spend enough time with him. Also, his father and I don't get along. We argue a lot. I don't trust him with my son. I don't like it, but I am civil and do share custody with his father.

Rachel is 20 years old and is originally from Cannon Falls, Minnesota.

My Best Friend
James Lee Carmichael, Saint Paul

This is the story of my best friend. James and I grew up in Pichard, Alabama. We did everything together; we would pick berries and knock pecans off pecan trees so my godmother could make pecan pies. We had a rough childhood, growing up. In Alabama it was different, desegregation had begun. James and I were separated. I was bussed to a school called Glendale High. It was an all white high school, and racism was very much alive. James was bussed to a school called Chickasaw High. Both schools were 1st through 12th grade. At the end of the day I would get on the bus and come home. I couldn't wait to see my friend James. I would ask him how his day was at school. Did he play any games with the other kids? He'd look at me and lower his head and start crying and say they called him names. I would ask, "What kind of names did they call you?" He told me, and I would start crying because it hurt his feelings and mine. We told our parents, and they would hold us and kiss our foreheads and tell us that we're beautiful.

I was in the third grade, James was in the fourth. James didn't like his school very much, and he would ditch school. Well, that didn't sit too well with the school. So they sent the police after him. James got caught and they sent him to farm school. Farm school was rough; they would beat him for not going to school. The little town of Pichard wasn't very big and James didn't want to go to that school, so I hid him in the barn, in back of the house.

When they came looking for him, they found my friend. He was my only friend, my best friend. I cried when they took James away because deep down inside I knew I wouldn't see him again. Reports came to James's mother saying he had run away, but we knew better. A week had passed and we hadn't heard anything. Then a letter came. The letter stated your son has been found, but not alive. My friend was dead; he had been hung on a cross down in the wooded lanes, a place where no one went.

James was my friend, and I loved my friend, even till this day. I will always think of him and miss him until the day I die. I love you James Green.

James Lee Carmichael is 50 years old and is originally from Pichard, Alabama.

I Could Never Forget My Auntie Hattie May Piers
Sade Bausley, Saint Cloud

I will never forget Ms. Hattie May Piers, she is my great-aunt. Hattie is an African-American woman who has inspired me. I still remember her saying "You should have another piece of my apple pie." We used to sit there and eat all day long. Aunt Hattie and I always had lots of fun together.

Aunt Hattie would always sit right next to me as I was having a hard time sleeping as a kid. She would just rub my head until I would fall asleep. I really do miss her. I don't think I will ever forget my Aunt Hattie. I also could never forget when she would brush my hair; then I would turn around and brush hers. Oh what fun that was. We would laugh at how tender-headed we both were. I just couldn't ever forget our summers we shared.

We both could feel if we were having a bad day. So we would comfort each other. I would kiss her rosy pink cheeks and squeeze her so tight. Then she would tell me how much I brighten up her days. I also can't ever forget her pound cake. She made it knowing it was my favorite.

Aunt Hattie would always say, "You are my favorite niece and never be afraid to ask me for anything you may ever need." Aunt Hattie would sit out in the yard on our swing and sing gospel songs in the afternoon summer sun. That's what inspired me to sing more. I learned all kinds of old songs from the slavery days. My aunt Hattie is a strong Black woman. She will always hold a special place in my heart.

In conclusion, I would like to say Aunt Hattie is a person I could never forget. In the past she gave me hope to say that I have a real family. My aunt Hattie isn't my birth family, she is on my adopted family side. She welcomed me and gave me my first chance in my life. I felt love and that is thanks to her. She gave me the attention that I needed all my life that no one has ever given me. When I needed a hug to say, "I love you, how was your day?" She was that person that I needed as a child with behavior problems. As of now I can't hug her anymore, but I have one thing that can never be taken and that's our memories we had together. That's why I could never forget my Aunt Hattie May Piers.

Sade Bausley is originally from Chicago, Illinois.

My Family
Felipa Islas, Minneapolis

My family is big and very beautiful. My parents are Cirila and Salvador. There are six siblings—five women and one man. I have two daughters and one son. They are Karla, Fernanda and Carlitos. Karla is thirteen years old. She is tall and thin. Her hair is long, straight and black. Her eyes are black. She is studying at the secondary school. She is intelligent and very pretty.

Fernanda is ten years old and is studying at the primary school. Her hair is medium length, brown and wavy. She is also intelligent, thin, and very funny.

My son, Carlitos, is my baby. He is the smallest of the three. He is small, thin, and has black short hair. He is studying at the primary school and is always playing football with his cousin and his friends. I love all three of my children with all my heart.

I also have three nieces and six nephews. That is all my family, and I hope I will be with them very, very soon in Mexico.

Felipa Islas is originally from Mexico.

My Best Friends
Raad A. Ahmad, Columbia Heights

I have two good friends. They share some of the same personal qualities. One characteristic I like about my friends is that they are responsible.

One friend is Safaa. He was a very nice friend. I am very sad now because he is dead. Safaa had an honest heart. He worked with me on the trade and helped with all business. I remembered his words in the hard work in my life that are most valuable: love, friend, confidence. My other friend is Hassan. He lives now in Jordan. He is a very nice friend.

He has the same characteristic qualities with me and Safaa. Before, he helped me in our business and now he looks after my business in Iraq alone, because I can't travel to Iraq in this time. He takes care of my job in Iraq. I value my two friends who are both my fortune. They are my pride in this life.

A Moment in Time
Armando Bryant, Rochester

I was trapped, captivated by her stare; a stare I had met time and time over. This stare I had come to know as God's personal blessing to me. She was an angel sent to me to show me the meaning of love and how to love. But her stare was not the same; a once confident young lady whose eyes would show no fear, now seemed weak, vulnerable. These same eyes were now equipped with tears and a deep sense of horror. I could not help but cry along with her as I saw her beautiful face turn pale with tears streaming uncontrollably down her face. Her once jade eyes no longer carried the vibrant glow of the morning light; instead appearing a deathly shade of grey that tore my soul apart. I couldn't do it. I couldn't find the words I knew she waited so desperately to hear; words of comfort, to ease the pain, to stop her tears. "Everything is going to be fine, sweetheart. Please don't worry. Just remember, no matter what, you are forever and always my love."

Words I find so simple now were lost to me at the time. I had no way of expressing myself. My heart was caught in my throat, allowing neither words nor sound to escape. My world seemed to be collapsing around me as I looked into her eyes. They seemed to tell me a story of a tragic end of her love and I had no way of reassuring her. I didn't know what was to become of us. I had no knowledge if I was going to return to her. So we just sat there as they rushed up the stairs to take me. We sat there, everything in the world slowed by the pain in her eyes. I tried so hard to muster up control of myself to tell her. I knew that she knew I loved her, but I wish I could have told her, "I love you, Jace."

I Remember My Grandfather
María Ochoa, Minneapolis

I remember growing up in my country, in Guatemala. I lived with my mother, my grandfather, three sisters and one brother. My father worked far away; he sometimes stayed home. He drove buses. I remember my grandfather bringing the toys. He asked me, "Do you like big toys or small toys?" I said, "I like big toys. My brother likes small toys."

I went to walk with my grandfather. One day, we went to the store. He bought one soda and two breads. I became tired. My grandfather said to me, "Sit and drink the soda and eat the bread."

I was ten years old when my grandfather died; it was very hard for me. I will always remember my grandfather in my life. My dream with my grandfather was when I was fifteen years old. I danced with him at my party. I remember my grandfather—for me, he never died. He lives in my heart, so I will never forget him. He made different games to play in the yard for my brother and me. He played violin and guitar and tried to teach me. Right now, when my two daughters and my son play guitar, I remember my grandfather.

Singing Songs for Mom
Yassamin M., Coon Rapids

My mother was born in Iraq. My mother is very white; you can see the veins in her hands and neck. When I was small, I always remember my mom was missing her mom a lot. She was always singing a sad song, because she could not see her mom.

After I was born, we had to leave Iraq because of political reasons. My mom could not see her mom or talk to her by phone. After 25 years, her mom died. My mom is a very nice person; she never fights and always forgives everybody.

I remember when I was a kid my mom made very nice dresses for me. Everybody was amazed, and she cooked very well. Everybody liked her cooking, but now she misses me a lot, and I don't like to see her in pain. It is very expensive for me to visit her, but I try my best to visit her once every two to three years. I miss her too, and now I sing sad songs the way mom used to sing for her mom.

My Family Members I Lost
Kadiatu Bah, Saint Cloud

My father was my best friend, but he died, so I missed him a lot. After one year, my mom died too. A couple months later, my sister passed away, and after a year, my husband died. So I lost all of my people I cared about. I am so sad and lonely but am glad I have two daughters. They make me busy all the time, and they love me. But I wish to have a good person in my life to love me and my two girls. This is my story right now.

A Scary Morning
Anonymous, Hopkins

Two years ago, my 18-month-old son and I lived in a townhouse in downtown Hopkins. It was a spring morning. As usual, we woke up and went downstairs and I started to prepare breakfast. After we finished eating, I dressed my son in his warm clothes, because it was raining. I tried to wash my dishes and got a call from my friend and started to chat with her. While I was talking to my friend, my son unlocked the door and then left. After one minute, I saw that the door was open and immediately I realized that my son was lost. I was very scared. Luckily, I found him right away. I will never forget that really scary morning!

My Childhood Memories
Marco, Minneapolis

I still remember some memories from my mother. She was the most wonderful mom in the world. She always took care of my brothers, my sisters, and me. She provided food, clothes, good education, and anything she could get for us. I was always waiting for my mom to go to sleep, as I was the baby of the family. She was happy most of the time. Mom helped anywhere people needed her.

She also liked to sing. In the morning, she used to turn on the radio and sing along while she was doing her duties. Sometimes she got angry, because I didn't follow her rules, but I still loved her. One day, she got sick and passed away. It was Friday night; we were watching TV in the living room and she started to feel sick. Then, my older brother took her to the hospital, but when they got to the hospital, she died. At that time, I was only twelve years old. Nobody told me anything had occurred, but I could notice that something bad was happening. Everybody was crying and getting ready for the funeral. I couldn't cry, but I was feeling so sad all the time. It is so hard when you lose your mom, and you are twelve years old. Your thoughts and life change completely.

So, if you have your mother with you, tell her how much you love her and take care of her. Also try to spend more time with her, because your mother is the most important person in your life.

WHEN I WAS PROUD OF MYSELF

Most of the time people are proud of themselves for many reasons. Some people are proud of what they have achieved and others of efforts they went through. In my situation, the first time I felt deeply proud of myself was the day I found a little baby near the trash. I would like to share the story of the little baby and how I found the baby. One day, I was walking nearby our house in Mogadishu, Somalia. I heard the sound of a baby crying, and immediately I stopped walking, and I tried to listen carefully.

When this happened, I was thirteen years old. It was not easy for me to come to the place right away because I was so scared, but I was very interested to know what was going on. I tried hard not to be scared, because I was so curious to see what was there. I came closer to the trash area, and I saw a baby lying down near the trash. The baby was wrapped with a piece of cloth, and the baby was crying so badly.

I thought the baby's mother was around. I looked in every direction to make sure. After I looked around and didn't see anybody, I knew the baby was alone. I grabbed the baby, and I took the baby to my mother who was at home at that time. I told her about what I found. When she heard my loud voice, she came out from the house, and she asked me what happened. "Why are you screaming?" I said to her, "Look, I found a baby."

After mother put the baby on her lap and tried to change the baby's clothes, she knew the baby was a baby boy. My mother was so happy that the little baby found her. She started to give him a bath while I was preparing his milk. My mother gave him milk, put him on a clean cloth, and he drank milk, and stopped crying. She kept comforting him. My mother sang a baby's song, and the little boy went to sleep.

My mother took care of the boy, and he is my brother, and I love him so much. That was the time I was deeply proud of myself because most children my age can't do that, so it makes me so happy when I remember because I think I was so brave.

Sharifo Ali has lived in the United States for 18 years. She was born in Somalia but lived in Kenya for two years before coming to the USA at age 20. Three of her teenage children live with her, but her oldest son lives with his father. Sharifo lives in Minneapolis and is training to be a census taker. Her goal is to be a nurse. She thinks the best part of coming to the United States is that there are more opportunities, and the hardest part is being a single mother, which is more difficult than most people understand.

Life as a Single Mom
Brittany Lehman, Saint Paul

When I was young, I always pictured myself being with the love of my life, having a child, and being able to support myself. A few years have gone by now, and it seems like a blink of an eye. I am 21, a high-school dropout and a single mother living at home with my parents.

I never pictured life to be this way, but I love being a mother. I wouldn't change it for anything. When I found out I was pregnant, I was in a relationship and my boyfriend and I were very happy to be expecting. During my pregnancy, I soon found myself alone and living back home with no job. I was very scared. My baby's dad was there when I had my son and for the first few months after. I then ended up in a violent relationship and had to get away.

I moved in with my parents and looked into getting my GED. My son is now 17 months old. I go to school at the Family Learning Center for my GED. I have passed two tests and am getting ready to pass my third. My son is the highlight of my life. He also goes to school with me and attends the children's program. I love that I am doing something to benefit my life, such as getting my GED. Now I am looking toward my future. I am looking for a job and soon looking forward to getting my GED. I also plan to have my own place to live—a place for my son to call his own. Being a single mother is hard, but it is all in the way you make it out to be. I am a single mother and proud to say that. I know I do a great job at being the mother that my son needs.

My Husband
Anonymous, Minneapolis

I'm from Ecuador. I came to the U.S. in 1999. This country is different from my country. I like to live here, but my life is very sad, because I lost my husband.

One day on a holiday, my family, friends, husband and I went to the park close to Wisconsin. That park had a river. When we went there, we cooked and played. It was 11:30 a.m., and my husband, friends and brothers went swimming. Suddenly, everybody was crying. I went to ask where my husband was. Nobody said anything. Then somebody said, "Your husband is dead." It was so bad. Everybody went out of the water except my husband. He drowned. After the accident, my life is very sad.

Do Your Best
Miguel Tamayo, Crystal

When I think about my father, I think about my fondest childhood memories. I started playing soccer when I was in first grade. I was probably the worst player on the team. I am sure my dad must have known it, but he never let on. I continued to play soccer for many years. I was never very good, but my father always supported me. He always said, "I am proud of you. You are my champion." That time, I felt comfortable and happy, although I was not the best one on the team.

When I was a child, we spent most of our vacation on the beach and lake. It was in my country, but my dad always worked hard during the year and he tried to save money.

My father taught me to be responsible, honest, trustworthy, and to respect all life. He taught me how to make good decisions in life, how to face any problems in life, and how to have a positive attitude and be strong.

My father has had a great influence on

my life. When I was a little boy, my father always hugged me and said, "Do your best." My father's advice is, "Believe in God and think like a winner." He believed in me one hundred percent and that gave me confidence. I am an adult now. My father still hugs me and says, "Do your best."

Thanks Dad.

The Best Food for My Family
Sabina Tabukum, Coon Rapids

We have many kinds of food in the U.S., but the best for my family is rice and stew. I cook it about four times a week before any other kind of food. Rice is also easy to prepare, but it has many styles for cooking. My family likes to eat rice every day. I wish to make them happier by cooking what they want.

Sabina Tabukum is originally from Cameroon, West Africa.

Hard Dreams
Carmen C. Rodríguez, Eagan

I will never forget how badly I wanted to come to Los Angeles when I was 16 years old. That was my big dream. The truth was that my sister lived in Los Angeles, but she never told me how she lived. She was always sending money and things to support us. I never imagined the life she led. I was thinking it was nice. When I came, she paid for everything for me—plus the rent. She didn't tell me anything. Five months later, somebody told me she paid everything for me, but she was only working part-time. She did not want to tell me that she was not working full-time. Sometimes she left the house telling me that she was working, but she just walked around the streets to be out of the house and let me believe she was at work. I felt bad. I talked with her and she told me, "I don't want you to suffer." Well, I was thinking about her feelings, so I made the decision to return to Mexico to get married.

Later, my husband and I moved to Minnesota with no money, no family, and no jobs. We arrived in February. The first three weeks, we slept on the floor, covering ourselves with a big towel. One day, a good person visiting us gave us a mattress and a blanket. After three months, my husband found a job. He soon worked three jobs and I went to ECFE classes and worked one job. After three years of hard work, we bought a house in Mexico for my parents, sister, and three brothers. Then we bought a house in Minnesota for our family where we live with our three children. Finally, after nineteen years of working and raising children, I have the opportunity to study English. I have very good teachers and friends in my life. My dreams are coming true.

Carmen C. Rodríguez is originally from Mexico.

Every Morning
Verónica River-Arteaga, Shakopee

Every morning is the same: Hurry!! Every morning, I'm running. It doesn't matter how much I prepared the night before; we never have enough time. I just wake up and my oldest son starts the day by making the youngest cry. "Get dressed! Make your bed!" I say, while I'm putting on my makeup and changing the baby's diapers. Then it's time for breakfast, and while I'm cooking they are running or singing or playing another noisy game. "Breakfast is served, come here!" I say, and after a few seconds for sure I hear: "Oh! Mom, we hate this, I wanna eat that!" But after a little explanation about why, for today, this is the best option, they finish their breakfast and ask me for more. Always, their lips show what they were eating, or they finish showing a big moustache with chocolate or juice. They look so cute!

"OK. Now it's time to wash your teeth and let's go to the bus stop." We are on time, with lunch and everything in their backpacks. We walk to the bus stop, but their little steps don't help us to advance, so I must lift the youngest to be on time. We pray while walking, and we say goodbye to the oldest. I drop off the youngest with his babysitter. Now I'm driving to my English school, everything is so quiet... I can't wait until they come back—I miss them so much. I love their noise, their faces, their laughs—they make me happy.

It's hard, this being a Mom, but every morning I know: I'm blessed to have these little ones next to me!

Verónica River-Arteaga is originally from Mexico.

"Sorry, I Can't Do It"
Long Le, Inver Grove Heights

My family came to the U.S. in August 2009. I decided to live in the U.S. because of my children's future. My children were good students in their school in Vietnam, and I hope they will be better than most of the students in the U.S.

In the first days, we were stressed out because our life changed a lot. I knew that, so I told my daughter, "Don't worry, darling! The first trimester just adapt yourself to circumstances. Do your best and get on top in the second trimester." But after the first exams, my daughter came home and said, "Sorry, I can't do it. Daddy, I can't wait any longer. I got the best grade of my class!!!"

My burden is becoming lighter and lighter every day.

My Life
Janice Thompson, Minneapolis

My name is Janice S. Thompson. I was born in Chicago, Illinois, mostly raised in Minneapolis, Minnesota. My parents' names are Monique Jefferson and Lamar Thompson. I have one older brother and two younger sisters. I also have two nieces, one from each sister. I have a two-year-old daughter who I love more than anything.

I was born November 14th, 1990 in Cook County. My mom was there visiting and happened to go into labor with me. Later, my mom returned home to Minneapolis with my brother and me. What I remember most is my first day of school. I was so happy to be around so many kids my age. I attended the School of Extended Learning, which is now Jordan Park. Then we moved to Chicago where I attended Caldwell Academy.

I was so elated when we moved back to Minnesota. I then attended Loring for a year. After there, I went down the street from my house to Cityview. Cityview to me is important because that is where I met some of my best friends. Their friendships meant more to me than any of my other friendships. Danielle, Andrea, Mariah and Quimarra are their names. We were so close that you never saw one of us without the others.

Now high school was very different. We all attended separate high schools. As for me, I went to North Community High School. I really didn't make new friends because I felt I already had enough friends. Later on in the school year, at the age of sixteen, I became pregnant. I worked very hard to finish the school year. I knew from then on that things weren't going to be easy for me.

In September of 2007, I gave birth to my beautiful baby girl, Aniya. My life was changing right before my eyes. I was now a full-time mom and student. At that time I was a student at Augsburg Fairview Academy. Things were very difficult, but I worked hard every day. I knew I had to succeed for a better future for my daughter and me.

I am now a student at Northside ABE classes. I plan to graduate by June of 2010. I also work full time as a Personal Home Care Assistant. I plan to get my GED and go on to college. I want to be a nurse by the time I'm 25.

My Family
Ayan Mohammed, Minneapolis

I was born in Hergesa, Somaliland in 1982. I came to the United States in 2008. I'm from a big family. I have ten brothers and four sisters, but my mother had only eight kids. My father had three wives. My father had a store in Hergesa. He used to sell clothes and gas. I remember my parents always loved each other.

One of Those Funny Days
Noe Pérez, Maplewood

I remember when I was about 12 years old; I was on the way to the farm with my cousin and two more brothers. In my country, Mexico, we use donkeys to carry stuff or to ride on. So that day, my lazy cousin decided to get a ride on the donkey, but when he pulled the donkey to the side of the street to jump on it, the donkey walked away and he fell down on the ground. So he got mad and wanted to cry, but he didn't. He started laughing, and we started laughing at him too. It was so funny that I can't forget that day.

Noe Pérez is originally from Mexico.

The Opportunity I Never Had
María Murray, Forest Lake

Every time when I am thinking about my mother I want to cry. She grew up with the responsibility of a mother. Her mother died when she was a young girl, and she was forced to make all the decisions in the family. Her father was sick and her brother was too little. Both lacked the ability to do it, so my mother sacrificed her life for the good of her family. Years later, my mother married. She had eight children and she was left with eight children to raise as a single mom. She worked hard to provide for the family. All my brothers went to school, but my mother thought girls need not to go to school.

My early education ended in the ninth grade. When my mother told me I had to leave school, I felt very bad and sad. I liked school so much. After I left school, I stayed in my house, only cleaning. After three years at home, I decided to leave the family because there was no future in my life.

My life after leaving the family was harder and more difficult. I married. I had four children. I left my husband because he was very irresponsible. I had to work very hard to provide for my family. Because of a lack of education, I had only bad jobs. I can't speak English. For many years, I worked hard.

Years later, I married again. I found my lovely husband who permitted me to go to school. I started learning a second language about a year ago. I have improved my language skills and now I am studying for a high school diploma in Forest Lake, Minnesota. I plan to enter a community college in the future. Now I have the opportunity that I never had before.

María Murray is 42 years old and is originally from Mexico DF.

All About Me
Jennifer Jackson, Minneapolis

My name is Jennifer Re'nee Jackson. I was born January 20th, 1988 to Sharon Jackson and Jerry Gray. I was raised in Chicago, Illinois on the Southside. I lived in Chicago up until I was fourteen years old. By that time my mom and her three kids moved to Minnesota. When we first moved to Minnesota, we stayed in Woodbury. Living out there with nothing but animals and unfamiliar people was kind of hard because there wasn't much to do. I say this because all there was was kids my age and a small park where everybody loved to go and hang out. Being the person that I am, I don't like being around too many people that I don't know. Once I got used to being out in Woodbury, I met this girl whose name is Amanda. Once I got to know her, she was the only one that I did talk to. One day we went to the park, the one that everybody loved to go and hang out. She introduced me to some of her friends. The ones that she introduced me to I really did not like because of their attitude. With my attitude and their attitude it was not going to work. When I started school out in Woodbury, I did meet a lot of people that I have gone to school with back when I was in Chicago. That was a good start for me. I got the hang of being around the people that I did not know.

How My Grandmother Took Care of Me
E.S.J., Saint Paul, for Celia Rivera Solis

I think a good person in my family is my grandmother, because she took care of me when I was a boy. She always was with me. That's why I chose her as a good person in my family. Also, she was a good cook, but now she is old and she can't do the things she was doing when she was a little younger. That makes me sad, but she is a good person. I think when she dies she is going to Heaven. But not yet because she is still alive. But my family and I are waiting for the sad moment and that makes me sad because I would like to have my grandmother forever. But I think it's impossible because we have to die one day.

My Life
José Angel Cortez, Minneapolis

My name is José Angel Cortez, and I would like to write my life history. I came from a big family—my parents, seven brothers, and four sisters. We are from Tijuana, Mexico. When I was a child, I remember that I was very happy living, playing, running, jumping and more with my family.

I remember the time to go to bed and to sleep every single night was so fun. I talked with my brothers, watched TV with my parents and slept. I remember, too, five brothers in the same bed playing until we slept. Another thing that I remember was that it was like living at a party every day. Some of my brothers ate breakfast and others took showers and cleaned the house. Imagine everybody sitting and eating at the same time. Impossible! Too many people! So my mom divided the sisters and brothers into shifts for breakfast, lunch, dinner, or whatever at different times. Six of us went to the middle school. I remember the bus driver couldn't believe picking up six brothers at the bus stop. If the bus was full, we couldn't leave two or three of my brothers. We were all on the bus or nobody was. Those are the best moments for reminders of my life. We were very poor, but very happy. We were without a nice house, car, or clothes, but we had big hearts.

Thank you.

Change
Carrie Thyes-Brown, Elk River

Long overdue
Painful but true
Not easy to face
I must do this now
And hopefully change for the better
I want to give my family more
All I can do is my very best
I am determined to become stronger and more focused
I will do all I can to accomplish my goals

Forever Is What He Said
April Romero, Cloquet

Forever is what he said
I see forever in his eyes
And that made me realize
That he's mine
For life

Forever is what he said
Being with him,
Sometimes it makes me feel like singing,
Because I know that he was meant to be
With only me
When I wear a wedding ring
And this won't be the end
Of my future dreams

Forever is what he said
I want to spend the rest of my life
Being his wife
This only feels right
Since he wants to be with me, too

Forever is what he said
He was my friend in the past
And I think that our relationship will last
I think this is the best

Forever is what he said
He loves me for who I am,
And I love him for who he is
We are each other's
Dreams come true

My Family
Hassan A. Aden, Minneapolis

Every weekend my family and I go to dinner.
When I am with them, I feel like a lottery winner.
My son and I usually order the steak with potatoes,
but my wife likes the salad with tomatoes.

After we eat our big meal, we like to eat some dessert.
When we are all done our stomachs sometimes hurt.
I love the weekends because we spend family time together.
It makes me so happy I always want to go out
on weekends even when there is bad weather.

After dinner we always go to the mall.
My daughter likes to shop; she bought a shawl.
Last weekend we went shopping for two hours.
We bought also some beautiful flowers.

When we got home we were so tired.
I wanted to drink some milk, but it was expired.

I drank some tea and I took a nap.
But my wife surprised me with a gift for me to unwrap.
I was so happy, she gave me a book to read.
I love my family. They always help people in need.
That's why they are good people. They do a good deed.

Hassan A. Aden is 71 years old and is originally from Somalia.

My Yearly Project
Shelly Gordien, White Bear Township

My name is Shelly Gordien. I'm the youngest of five girls. Every year, my older sisters have an idea of what to buy our parents. One year, about five years ago, I had a great idea to make a calendar. For my parents, I made a calendar of all my family members' birthdates and their best or their funniest picture of the year. One year, I collected baby pictures of all the kids. That was fun. I also put the wedding anniversaries on the calendar, but only the dates. My brother-in-law and my uncle passed away; but in their memory, I continue to put the date of their birthday on the calendar, but not a picture. I try to work on taking pictures all year long. So when I start working on the calendar, I can pick the best one. My family has nicknamed me the "Picture Nazi," but all in fun. Everyone loves the calendar and looks forward to seeing it at Christmas time. It is one of the highlights of the year. It is also a big part of my fall time. It is something I can give back to my family to enjoy all year around.

My Role Model
Daopeth Cida, Minneapolis

Chai is always my role model because he is very ambitious, patient, hardworking, and also intelligent. Though he was born in a poor family, he has never given up on studying. "Only studying can make me and my family have a better life," he said. Moreover, Chai's dream was entering the University of Laos.

I still remember that when we were in the same class in high school, we were very friendly, and we helped each other whenever we were in trouble. Chai was a good and outstanding student at any subject in my class. Chai could explain the lesson clearly to friends who were in a pickle. As well, Chai loved to read a lot; everybody called him "a bookworm guy." At the same time, he studied and worked to help his family. His parents were not able to work; they were getting old and his father had lung cancer. He was responsible for one younger brother and his parents. During our last grade of high school in 2004, Chai worked like a dog; he worked in a restaurant as a waiter and washed dishes in a bar. At that time he was up the creek; he had no time to do homework, sometimes he missed class, and final tests were coming. All his friends and teachers worried about him, because he was such a good student in our school. So Khamvan, who was the affectionate and kind principal of our high school, came over to his house to talk things over. She gave him a better way to manage his time. She hired him to take care of her garden only one to two hours per day so that he had time to keep his dream going. Finally, you know what happened? He got financial aid from the government to enter the university in Germany. That was a shock to everybody!

Chai's experiences have inspired me all the time whenever I've been in the same situation like him, and I will always tell myself, "Don't give up if you haven't done it yet. Just keep the ball rolling." One day soon, I look forward to getting my GED diploma so that I can enter college like he has.

Daopeth Cida is originally from Laos.

When a Dog Eats a Person
See Yee, Minneapolis

One day, a long time ago, my father and I went to the farm. Maybe I was 13 years old. I asked my father, "What happens in my culture if some person dies, and then you have an animal eat a dead person's hand or leg? What happens to their family in the future, because I heard my grandfather talk about this story a long time ago when a dog would eat a hand or leg of a dead person. But I think this happened 30 years ago."

My father said, "Yes, it did, before my father came to Thailand. My cousin lived in Laos, a small country in the mountains, in 1965. All the people got sick from bacteria, so bad in the country. The people died a lot, and then my cousin died on the farm. Maybe he got bacteria and was very hurt. He died and nobody saw him for the next two days. In the morning, a dog tried to eat his hand and leg, because the dog was very hungry."

"How about this, my father," I said. "A neighborhood is very scary. You get sick from bacteria all over the neighborhood. Then you have to move quietly because the Lao country had a problem with fighting from 1950 to 1975. This communism was in Laos. In the Hmong culture all the families had people who died from the war. What happened to all who died? Did the animals eat some people, so the people couldn't go on their way without the help of the shaman?"

"It's a long story, my son."

The Field Next to Our Home
Anonymous, Minneapolis

Every day after school, my brothers, all of our friends and I would come together to play soccer. When the game started, the dust blew all over the area and our faces would become brown. We would continue to play until the evening. When the sun set, my mother would come to call my brothers and me. Until then, we couldn't stop playing. The field was small for playing on but we would run over it like a big soccer field. We would make a group having two players each, and then we would play. Everybody in our village would gather by the side of the field waiting to enter, replacing the last group. While they waited, they used to clap for the person who played well or scored. That made it enjoyable and memorable for the village boys, even if it was small and full of dust.

History of My Father
Ahmed Abdullahi, Minneapolis

His name was Adam Abdullahi. He was born on June 5th, 1940 in Mogadishu, Somalia. My father was a shoemaker in his home. He had many customers and he was always busy. He started working at 6 a.m. in his house. He worked in his home for two years.

After two years, he started a small shoe factory near his house. People liked his shoes, because he made very good-quality and beautiful shoes. All the people liked my father.

He became a famous man in the village that he lived in. Some people suggested that

Da Her, Brooklyn Park

he start a big factory, so he would get more customers and more workers to supply the entire country with shoes.

My father wanted to start the biggest shoe factory in the country. He didn't have enough money, so he asked the government for a loan. The government did not give him the loan, so he continued to make shoes out of his small factory.

Ahmed Abdullahi is originally from Somalia.

My First PTO Meeting
Elizabeth Kong, Mankato

My first parent-teacher organization meeting made me very nervous and lonely. What made me nervous was that I didn't understand English well. The part where we had to introduce ourselves was hard for me. Imagine if you do not know the language how it would feel to talk in front of people.

Elizabeth Kong is 34 years old and is originally from Sudan.

Love Forever
Hang Dinh, Saint Paul

It was Mother's Day, but I didn't care or even know about it, because in my country we don't have that holiday. I woke up in the morning, and my son gave me a hug and said, "Happy Mother's Day! And today you don't have to do anything. Just relax or go somewhere else you like, and I have a surprise for you." And he gave me a card he made. I opened it. It was so cute with a picture inside and a note: "Thank you, Mom, for everything you gave me in my life and I love you forever." I can't describe to you all how happy I was. And my eyes suddenly got tears in them. I knew my Mom and loved her so much, but I never did anything to make her so happy, just like had happened to me.

Mother, I feel I am not a good child and I've been wrong to you. However, to make you happy and proud of me and to render thanks for giving birth to me and for raising me, Mom I promise to you, I will be a good model for my kids and will teach them to be helpful in the family and in the society like the ways you taught me. And I will take your grandkids and go back to visit you someday in the future.

Once again, thank you, Mom, for everything you gave in my life, and I love you forever.

Life Got Better
Mrs. Big Dottie, Saint Cloud

My name is Dorothy Beatrice Dawson Riley. I was born in Chicago, Illinois to Janie B. Dawson and Joseph Pugh. My mom lived in an apartment over a bar, and she had been drinking all day long and around six o'clock, she wanted to go up to rest. At 7:05 p.m. January 21th, 1969, I was delivered by my Aunt Dot whom my mom named me after.

I was taken from my mom at six months old because of neglect. I was placed in foster care with George and Lola Davenport, my wonderful mom and dad. I grew up in a little town outside of Chicago called Dixmoor, Illinois. We went to church every time the doors were open. I was placed back with my birth mom in 1975. A few months later, I was raped in a project elevator. The state sent me back to my mom and dad in Dixmoor, Illinois.

I stayed at least another year. Then I was sent back to my birth mom, and I was abused and raped two more times. At 14, I met my wonderful husband, Anthony Lewis Riley, and I told him I was 17 and he believed me.

Then two years later, I got pregnant and

Friends and Family - 105

had Anthony Lewis Riley Jr. on December 9th, 1985. He passed away from SIDS February 10, 1986. Then we conceived another son named Antonio Deshawn Riley born January 14th, 1987. He passed away from SIDS four months later as well. Then on August 17th, 1988, my husband and I had another son named Cortez. He is one of my miracle babies who almost passed away three times and is a healthy and smart adult as of now.

Soon after that, we conceived a baby girl on October 28th, 1990 named Cornequa, who is also a college student. In the same year, I got my son Jajuan. Then two years later, we adopted a baby girl named Shabrandy, who is a high school student and doing well for herself also. A year later, we conceived twins, one passed at first trimester of conceiving. Then soon after, I had Shaquanya, who was also sickly as a child and now is doing fine in high school.

We are proud parents of 11 children and four adopted children. I can really say my life turned out to be blessed with a great family.

Like a Bird in a Cage
Marisela Jaimes, Minneapolis

When I was six years old, my father brought me to the U.S. from Mexico, because my parents got divorced. I never got to see my mother again. At that time, my life was so unhappy that I used to feel so lonely and depressed. I felt like I was in a birdcage because I didn't have freedom. I was not allowed to have friends. Every day I was afraid, scared to come home from school because my dad would always be drinking and he would be violent. On my fourteenth birthday, instead of celebrating it, I was in a hospital because of a brutal beating from my father. At that time, I wanted to kill myself, but then social services took me to a foster home. I felt so lonely and sad, because of all the things that I had gone through. Now I see the world so differently, because I met a special person that came into my life. He showed me that the world is so beautiful even though he is not with me anymore. It's been thirteen years since that time, but my heart still has feelings towards him because he was my first love and because he saved my life.

Marisela Jaimes is originally from Morelos, Mexico.

The Hard Past, the Happy Future
Chaly, Brooklyn Park

In 2007, my husband and I came to Minnesota for a better future than in California. I came with my kids: Orlando, age three and Star, age two. I have another boy; he lives with my mom in Tijuana, Mexico. Alexander (age five) was born when I was in grade ten and I dropped out of school. In April 2008, my baby boy Isaac was born and at that time my husband had a good job, we had our own apartment and the future was looking cool. When my baby was three months old, I started to work and felt really good because I was helping my mom with good money for my son, Al.

My husband was taking care of the kids when I was at work and we took turns so we didn't have to pay a babysitter, but then the problems began with my husband—problems from the past. He decided to go back to California in December 2008. I decide to stay. Sometimes I start to feel that all the doors start to close to me because I have to leave my kids everywhere with someone to watch them. My mom is always asking me why I don't go back to California. I have all my family there, what I was doing so far away from home by myself? But sometimes friends can be better than family. I have to say that 2009 was a long, hard year with all my kids. But now I go to school and I do it by myself with my kids. Everybody gives opinions about what I should do, but nobody really knows the problems that I have.

Now we are in 2010 and I have my own place and I'm going to study hard to get my GED and everything is going to be better. I work at Wendy's but am looking for a better job. I know that one day my children are going to be proud of me. I wish that one day my son Alexander will come to live with me and his brothers and sister. I always say to my mom that I am going to stay in Minnesota even if it gets freezing cold. I miss so much the beach of my California but am okay by myself because I can do it. I am with my children now. I am divorced and my future looks cool again.

Thankful for America
Clarita Stiles, Inver Grove Heights

On December 25th, 1981, my friend arranged a blind date for me with a U.S. sailor. It was going to be a double date to attend the Christmas dinner aboard the U.S.S. Brooks, a Navy ship visiting my home country of the Philippines. My date was named Rod and he was supposed to pick up my friend and me and escort us on base as guests. He stood us up! We were very disappointed, but the next day Rod showed up to apologize for having cold feet. We started dating and were soon engaged before his ship left port three weeks later.

Rod petitioned for me to come to America using a fiancé visa. I arrived in Minnesota on June 21st, 1982, and we were married on June 30th. My journey was just beginning as together we raised two sons through college. They are both married and out on their own.

Now I am thankful to have this special chance to go to school. I prayed to God to show me how to get my education here in America and He answered my prayers. First, I attended English as a Second Language and now I am learning more in my new class. I am thankful for the United States for having an open door for people to come and receive an education and a new life. I also pray for the teachers who are so patient to help us learn as adults. I am very grateful for this program and pray that it continues to help many more people become successful in their new lives here in America. As I continue my journey, I hope to someday write a book about my story.

Clarita Stiles is originally from the Philippines.

My Childhood
Hafida Colley, Eagan

My name is Hafida Colley from Morocco in northern Africa. When I was a child, my parents used to buy new clothes for my brothers, sister, and me. The certain occasions when they would do this were religious feasts and annually when school started. We were very excited about that. Also, I remember my mother's mama visited us every Sunday and she brought with her toys for us. At this time, I was so delighted. She spent the whole day with us.

When I was four to five years old, I remember my cousin called me American girl because my hair was very blond like American women. Obviously, I never dreamed I would marry an American man and live in America. But I did. He converted to Islam, he became Muslim, and he is interested about Islam. Then we had a huge wedding in my country. I'm so lucky, because I married him without any issues about religion in either culture.

Annually, we have two religious feasts, one that follows Ramadan, a month of fasting. It is called Eid-al-Fitr in Arabic, which means Feast of Breakfast. The other is a great celebration of the most important religious holiday of the year. We call this great celebration Eid-al-Adha, which means Festival of Sacrifice. Muslims who can afford to do so sacrifice their best domestic animal, usually a sheep, but it could also be a camel, cow, or goat. This is good for us. I came here; I got a different life, my husband taught me and encouraged me a lot in my studies, driving, and history about the U.S. I appreciate him and God.

Hafida Colley is originally from Morocco.

My Daughter
Da Her, Brooklyn Park

One of the most important things in my life is my daughter. She is almost five years old now. My daughter, I can tell that she has the most amazing talents ever. We parents are very proud of her.

Inside of Me
Melaka Walton, Maplewood

Inside of me, there is a complicated person who I don't understand half of the time. There is pain, joy, frustration, and above all, confusion.

I escape in my music and let people hear it through my voice. When I get up on the morning, I take a shower, brush my teeth and pick out clothes that hug my body just right.

Inside of me, I am confused about so much. I am wondering why I am a single parent. Am I doing a good job? I think so because they are always smiling.

Inside of me, I am frustrated. I feel like I have no support with my kids. Sometimes I just need a break. That is what is inside of me.

Uncle Ray My Traveling Angel
Colleen Reinke, South Saint Paul

While you're driving
Down that lonesome highway
Hearing them truckers say
"Breaker One-Nine"
Zoning them out
To wonder if your family is fine
So you keep shifting those gears
To keep on rolling
Trying to finish this run
So you can call
And say "Hi"
And to tell your little one
"Sorry for all the days you missed throughout the years"

You do this all your life
So you can one day
Fly over the same roads
You once traveled
But now you are free
Free from the eighteen wheels
That once kept you down

I hope you're happy
Now that you are free
So please have peace
Flying over them mountains and seas
And be my traveling angel

My Wonderful Mom
Shamso Abshir, Minneapolis

My name is Shamso and I love my dear, sweet, amazing, intelligent, kind, caring mom. When I just see her warm eyes it makes me smile a thousand-dollar smile. It makes me thank God for giving me a mother who anybody would dream to have, and I wish I would be like her.

SUCCESSFUL WOMAN

I am a single mother who takes care of two children by myself. I work 40 hours a week and take care of my children at the same time. Living in America is not easy. I came to America with my family. When I came to America, I was 15 years old.

I went to high school for one year. In my second year of high school, my father arranged a marriage for me and I accepted the marriage. I got married and it worked well. After all that, I continued to go to high school. I did well in all my classes. When I told my teachers I was going to get married, they were happy for me.

When I got pregnant, I left high school because my pregnancy was difficult. After I had my first child, I went back to high school. After three months, I became pregnant again. After that, I never went back to high school again.

I stayed home to raise my children and had a wonderful life. My ex-husband was working and I was doing all the household work. After five years, I got divorced and I moved on with my life. When I became a single mother, my life started to be difficult and I struggled to raise my two beautiful kids.

Now my kids are grown up and I am a successful woman. I thank God for helping me through all the hardship and for giving me strength to help me raise my family.

Sabaha Sharif is from Somalia. She is a mother and has two beautiful children. She came to the U. S. in 2000. Her father came to the U.S. in 1997. After her dad came to the U.S., he sent visas to come to America. She came with her whole family. She went to high school, but she didn't graduate. She is a mother who works forty hours a week, and she loves to go to school. She lives in Minneapolis and goes to Franklin Learning Center (FLC) five times a week where she studies different subjects. If she works hard, she hopes to become a Nursing Assistant. She is proud to be in the United States. She thanks the FLC, her teachers, the college students who help her every day and her special tutor Douglas who has worked with her for over two years.

Friends and Family - 109

Personality
Shukri Abayle, Minneapolis

My personality as a child was playful. When I was a child, I liked to play outside. My parents and my relatives described me saying I was a good girl. My personality had changed when I got older because when I was a child, I didn't know right or wrong, but when I got older I do remember everything. When I was a child I was shy with strangers because I didn't know them. With the strangers I do remember one thing when visitors visited us, I ran into the bedroom. I didn't come out until visitors left.

Shukri Abayle is 28 years old and is originally from Somalia.

Dear Mom
Hadi Ali, Saint Louis Park

I will mention a little bit about my mom. First, she is the one who brought me into this world and taught me how to walk and how to speak my mother tongue. She made me the man I am today. She used to work hard for us.

As I was growing up, when I was young, back home, I did not like to wake up early to go to school. She encouraged me to go to school and study as well as I could. I am so proud of my mom. I do not know how I can reward her and make her happy all the time. I remember all the time the sweet words she used to say to me. When I think back on my childhood, I remember how well she treated me and raised me.

I want to say to everybody who is in this universe to make sure to take care of your mothers. We all appreciate our mothers. We know what mothers do for us, but I wonder why some people do not care for their mothers or make them happy. Some people do not even know where in the world their mothers live.

Mothers worry about their kids all the time. There are some mothers who study with me and their cell phones ring all the time. The rest of the students (who do not have kids) look around and wonder why their phones are always ringing. One of the students asked another why she didn't turn off her phone. The mother's answer was that she left her kids. When I heard the words she said, I felt sorry for her. So all I can say is God bless mothers.

Two Families
Kao Vang (A), Brooklyn Park

I was born to my first mom and dad. They lived in the mountains far from education and with no money. They had everything in the farm. They gave everything from the farm to support the family.

My second mother and father are my teachers. They have education and understand everything. They taught me, and right now I understand more about the United States. I thought and kept the good things to support my family, and I remember what the people told me forever.

Kao Vang (A) is originally from Laos.

A Memoir of My Mother for Mother's Day
MorMai Yang, Saint Paul

Take a moment to just think about all of the good things about your mother. Yer Lor, my beloved mother, was like a small house filled with lots of beautiful memories. She raised all her children well with the finest quality of love.

My dear mother was like a flowing river that has a special place to stay. The heart of this river is strong enough to carry all kinds of people, whether good or bad. Her living waters will support everything that draws from her. The purity within her cleanses all diseases. Yer Lor was the life that shines through, is even as the daylight that reveals the right path to follow in our own daily lives.

My mother taught me everything in life that I needed to know, one step at a time. She always knew exactly what level I was at even though I often ran ahead of her. Her kind patience and vast wisdom advanced me from one level of maturity to another. I am so thankful for her careful guidance.

Before my dearest mother departed from this world, she imparted three wonderful gifts to me. She gave me the gifts of teaching, cooking, and healing. In teaching, the best way she taught me was by being an example. For cooking, all her secret recipes are kept safe with me. Last, but not least, I'm able to heal myself and others with our traditional Hmong herb medicine that has been passed down from generation to generation.

My precious mother, Yer Lor, was the best mom I could ever ask for. She was the greatest teacher of life to me. She paved the right way for me, a sweet guiding light. She also taught me to become my own best friend whenever I failed. She gave me all her wisdom and strength to survive on my own in this complex world. Looking back and reflecting upon everything that my mother had taught me, I can confidently smile and say, "Thank you my darling mother for all that you've done for me. I love you."

MorMai Yang is 35 years old and is originally from Laos.

Sixteen
Diane Moss Baptiste, Columbia Heights

When I was 16, I had a job, my own apartment and one kid. My mother helped me raise him, and my mother spoiled him. I didn't have a 16th birthday party because my mother didn't have the money to give me party. Then I had a daughter when I was 19 years old, and my mother helped me to raise her. I didn't go to a bar. When I was 16 years old, I didn't go to house parties because they liked to fight there. I got married when I was young. When I got married my mother told me not to do it. Then I get pregnant and my mother told me it wasn't good to be married to him. Sixteen was my favorite age because it was the best time I had in my life. I liked to go to the store and shop for clothes.

My Father and My Mother
Heather Duong, Eagan

The person who has influenced me the most in my life is my father, Vinh. I admire my father for three reasons. First, his determination: He learned English very well and became a teacher. Second, he gives to charity: He likes to donate to the people who need help. Third, he always encourages us to learn more English.

No matter how busy he is, he doesn't forget to be concerned about our education and his volunteer job for charity. He has had a very positive influence on my life.

My mother is a wonderful person! She is a homemaker. She has seven children: five girls and two boys. I'm the third. When we were little, she had to do everything. She went to the market every day, washed a lot of clothes by hand and helped us take baths.

She taught us how to be good people and to have respect for ourselves. She helped us to do our homework. Whenever we had a problem, she was always there for us, listening, giving good advice and consoling us. My mother liked our friends, and we always played and hung out together as we grew up.

No matter how old we are, my mother always worries and is concerned about us! We always had a roof over our heads and food on the table, because she was dedicated to her family.

Myself and My Story
Marites Burnett, Saint Louis Park

I'm not a degree holder. I'm just an ordinary person. I was born in Malangas, Philippines, the place called the land of black gold. Why? Because we had a carbon or coal mine. Some people said my country is one of the lucky places in the world, because the plants are easy to grow and there are a lot of fruit plantations and beautiful beaches. Anyway, my name is Marites Burnett. My husband is American. I came here to Minnesota a day after my birthday—December 17th, 2007. I will never forget. It was winter time, my first experience of snow. I ran outside and played and then I ate some of the snow flakes.

I say my lifestyle had big changes because it's a lot different from before. I'm normally busy—I go to work every day. But now I'm still busy taking care of my baby and my husband—new place, new mom.

I miss my family so much in my country. But I'm happy because my new family here loves me so much and they welcome me in my husband's family. I love Minnesota—I don't like the cold here, but I love the snow. Right now I'm getting my English lesson to improve my English language, because I want to teach my baby and understand and talk to my husband properly. And also I plan to continue learning to get a better job some day. My baby right now is one year old. We have a lot of plans for him. For me, I want him to go to school and study hard because education is very important.

My Best Friends
Nghiem Nguyen, Coon Rapids

I have two best friends. With me, they are very best friends. One characteristic I like about my friends is that they often come to me when I have big problems.

My first friend is Gan. He is living in Vietnam. He often helped me in my life, gave me some very good advice when I was there.

My second friend is Thanh. He is living in Brookyn Park. When I had just come to the U.S., I was very sad. Sometimes I wanted to go back to my country. He often advised me, helped me with some things and he helped me find a job. I got a good job until today.

Thanks a lot to them. I'll never forget them in my life.

My Best Friends
Fadumo Sulub, Fridley

I have two friends. One's name is Kadra. She is very good and she graduated from her university five years ago. We have known each other about six years. She was my bridesmaid, and she always helps me, especially when my son was in the hospital. She came and saw him every day, and she was bringing me food and whatever I wanted. She is very happy and very friendly.

My other friend's name is Sahra. She is a Metro North student. We met three months ago when she started school. She didn't know how to say "A, B, C," but now she is level three and she knows how to speak English, read and write. She is very successful.

My Undesired Trip
Kadar Abdi, Minneapolis

In December 1990, civil war broke out in Mogadishu, Somalia. It was midterm of my first semester in high school. During this time, I had no choice but to leave the city. My whole family split and lost one another. It was such a desperate time in my life. I fled by lorry to Kismaayo, the southern side of my country, with my uncle. The trip to Kismaayo was remarkably terrible. We had no food, no water, nor any kind of emergency supplies.

We arrived in Kismaayo safely, but with nothing left in our hands. Those days still have a deep feeling in my memory. We started to look for shelter, a place to live, and human necessary things. After hard searching, we found a place to stay temporarily. It was an unsuitable place, but better than nothing. We started recovering from the despair of our trip. Suddenly, a fight and civil war started in Kismaayo, the place where we preferred to stay temporarily. That was another unfortunate time and the beginning of our stress. After three days of fear, we fled to the border of Somalia and Kenya. Although we suffered, we crossed the border safely to the Kenya side. That was my first undesired trip.

Kadar Abdi is originally from Somalia.

Levi Smith, Babbitt

Coming to America
Shamso Mohamed, Minneapolis

My name is Shamso. I came from Africa. I am 30 years old and married. I have children: two girls and one boy. Also, I have a husband. I love him, also, he loves me. I am very sad, because he is in Africa. When he comes to me, I am very happy. I miss my love and my children. If I get money, I will go to Africa. I miss my children and my sweet. Also I dream of my family now. I am working so I have money. I will go to Africa.

Shamso Mohamed is originally from Somalia.

My Life Before and Now
Mai Vang, Minneapolis

I was born in Thailand on September 13th, 1976. I had two brothers and nine sisters. My family lived in Bannayow nine years ago, because in 1985, no people lived in Bannayow. Some people decided to come to the US, but some people decided to go to Banvinai. My family decided to go to Banvinai too.

My family next moved to Banvinai in 1985. I was fourteen years old when I got married in January 1991 in Banvinai. Next, my family moved to Tamkrabot in 1992. In 2005, my family wanted to come to the United States. My family came to the U.S. on July 6th, 2005. My family lived in Portland, Oregon for seven months. My family moved to Minnesota on February 9th, 2006. Now I have six children—five boys and one girl. Now I live in North Minneapolis.

Mai Vang is 33 years old and is originally from Thailand.

Friends and Family - 113

Differences Between Generations
Yenanesh Keryo, Minneapolis

My parents' generation in the 1940s and 1950s was very different from my generation in the 1990s. There are lots of differences between these two generations including cultural, economical, and educational differences.

First, I heard from my parents that in their generation, they were more cultural or traditional when compared to my generation. For instance, if a guy liked a woman and wanted to marry her, he wouldn't go directly to her and ask her. He and his father had to send three or more wise people to the woman's parents' house. The woman's parents had some qualifications such as if the guy had some money, property and cows, oxen or ships. If the guy passed this requirement, they wouldn't ask any more questions. Even if the guy was very old and asked to marry a 13- or 14-year-old girl, they would let him marry without the young girl's permission. In my generation, things have changed. Girls all have the right to choose their future husbands without their parents' permission.

The second change is with the economy. In my parents' generation, to get a small amount of money, you had to work hard, but you could get things for very small prices. There were lots of available jobs for everyone. Most of the workers were men, because women didn't work—they stayed home and took care of the babies and the home. In my generation, getting money isn't easy and you can't get things cheaply. The number of unemployed people is high. Women also work. Even though there is a lot of new technology, the economy is shrinking every day. The economy in my parents' generation was better than in my generation.

The third change is in education. In my parents' generation, there were fewer chances for anyone to get an education, especially women. Many of the jobs women were able to get only asked for experience. In my generation, things have changed, and everyone has to go to school in order to get a better job. The longer we stay in school, the better pay we will get. There are only a few jobs that only ask about experience. These are the differences in being educated and not between my parents' generation and mine.

In conclusion, there are many differences between my parents' generation and my generation including cultural, economical, and educational differences.

My Dream
Marilyn Lodermeier, Saint Louis Park

I grew up in a poor family. We didn't have our own house. We didn't have television or a refrigerator, but we did have a radio to listen to the news. Anyway, when I was a kid, I had a big dream to become a newscaster or pilot to help my mom and dad survive; we have a big family. I have four sisters and six brothers. One day, when I got back from swimming, I felt somebody hit my head. It was like a huge big rock coming from the other hand and hitting my head. My mom was shocked. I cried loud and I asked for help. My mom took me to the doctor, and the doctor give me a pain medicine, and they took me to the x-ray machine to find out what was going on with me. Everybody was shocked when they found I was diagnosed with stage four tumor in my head and was going to have cancer. I am just the kid with a simple dream for my family. Now I am here, full of dreams, waiting for the miracle.

A Funny Memory Before I Was 10 Years Old
Faviola Estrada, Richfield

When I was young, I remember we always went to the beach with my mother. My father didn't live we us; he always stayed in the USA. But one day he came back and my mom said to us, "We need to change the city. We need to follow your father to his city."

I began elementary school, but I didn't have friends because I was new and everybody laughed. They said it was because I spoke funny, and they called me "chica fresca" because my accent was different from their accent. I didn't say anything because I was afraid. But now I laugh when I remember my childhood. It was funny for me because this time will never ever come back, and I will never seem the child again.

Faviola Estrada is 35 years old and is originally from Mexico.

My Parents as My Heroes
Florence Iketalu, Brooklyn Park

My heroes in my life are my parents. They brought me up in this world to become somebody that will be recognized in the society. When I was young, they sent me to school in order to learn how to read and write (education). They taught me all the necessary things I need in this world to become a human being. They brushed me up so that in the future, I would know how to be on my own.

They taught me how to respect people everywhere I go on earth. They did not lead me astray. They made me realize that in this world, you will struggle to become somebody in life. Anytime I started to be bored in school, my parents came and asked me, "How do you do in school?" I told them that I am bored. They started to give me words of encouragement. They told me that I would achieve my goal in life. They said to me, "Keep trying, one day you will make it." After their words of encouragement, I did not give up. My parents prayed for me not to be discouraged with my education. They said, "Education is the key to success." When they mentioned to me about success in education, I felt relaxed and started studying harder. My mother taught me how to cook, clean house, do laundry, wash dishes and so on.

Without my parents, I would not be here on earth. God gave them strength to make me be in existence in this world, especially in my education. Because of lots of encouragement in my education, I did not give up. In fact, any time I did not go to school, I was bored. I make it a point of duty that I will be going to school to learn more about things that will warrant me to be useful in this world. Education will help me get a good job that will yield money for me to prepare a living. I am working on my GED. I have passed two tests already.

Thanks for my parents. Once again, "Education is the key to success."

My Childhood
Andrei Abayeu, Anoka

When I was a child, I was very happy, because my parents loved my sister and me. My family spent a lot of time together. My father was a serviceman, therefore my family often moved to a new place. This was very interesting for my older sister and me. I had many new friends. Usually every summer we traveled to my grandmother. She lived in the Caucasus. My childhood was happy.

Shane -n- Candy
Shane Paige, Bloomington

Candy I want you 2 know I understand
Why your emotions -n- feelings u do not show
But Candy my dear, have no fear
Cause I am here -n- my love 4 u is real -n- sincere
So hold me near my dear -n- I'll never hurt you
Or make you shed a tear -n-
If you shed a tear it will be tears of joy,
When you have a beautiful baby boy.
Then you'll say Sure my dear,
I can see you are sincere.
I will no longer live in fear
My feelings -n- emotions are clear
Thank you my dear.

The Woman I Love
Alfred Einberger III, Rochester

She loves music, loves to dance.
I am sitting here waiting, hoping for a chance.
Beautiful days, beautiful ways,
I get lost, deep within her gaze.
Hair like silk, eyes like fire,
My love for her burns, like a funeral pyre.

Man of perfection, I am surely not.
Yet she puts up with me, from the bottom to the top.
Friends before lovers, friends to the end,
I pray our true love reaches no end.
She keeps me in wonder, she keeps me in awe.
Her dogs love me, they give me a paw.

Only a strong woman can stand by her man,
Picking up the slack wherever she can,
The days I've been gone, God has kept her along.
I know her words are true, when she says, "I miss you."
She has a soul that flies like a snowy white dove.
This is my woman, the woman I love.

My Dream
Yia Yang, Minneapolis

I have a dream that one day I will be a good old lady.
I have a dream that someday my son will get to be a doctor.
I have a dream that one day this country will have jobs.
I have a dream that one day all people in the world will not fight.

Yia Yang is originally from Laos.

My Uncle Is My Role Model
Houa Yang, Minneapolis

My Uncle Pao is my role model. When he was in the camp in Thailand, he worked hard and was a very good model for whole families. When he was young, he had to learn Hmong culture. Hmong culture is not easy, and nobody wants to learn it. My Uncle Pao was concerned about our culture, so he decided to take his time to learn it. Every night, he had to learn with his father-in-law. After that, he also had to be responsible for his family. He studied almost two years before he finished his class, but he thought it wasn't enough for him. He continued to practice with another teacher until he knew all about Hmong culture. He volunteered to help some people who didn't know about Hmong culture. He became very famous during that time and still is. All Hmong know him, especially old people.

He's our leader. He is very generous and will help with almost everything. That's why my whole family respects and listens to him. I remember when I first saw him. I was seven years old. He was very famous at that time. I thought someday he would be my teacher. We lived together in the camp in Thailand for fifteen years. In 1992, he decided to spend his life in the U.S. and left us soon after that. I didn't think I had a chance to see him again in my life. After he left us, we still lived in Thailand for almost thirteen more years, until in 2003 when the United Nations offered a program for us to come to the U.S. too. I was very happy because my dream was coming true, and I would see him soon. My Uncle Pao is my sponsor. I was so happy! In 2004, I came to the U.S., and when I saw him, my tears dropped down on by face.

Jerome Burks, Saint Paul

James Becerra, Rochester

Travel and Adventure

The Best Vacation
Diane Yanacheak, Saint Paul

The best vacation I have ever been on was when we went on an airplane and flew to Florida. We rented a car, and it was a Mustang car. So we put the top of the car down in the middle of November. It was great. We drove down to our hotel, and we had a room that looked over the pool and ocean. So we both tried snorkeling, but Art did better than I did. I didn't know how to swim, so I went back on the boat. I was very cold, so I stayed on the boat. When we got back to shore, I went to my room and got warm clothes on. I was freezing. Then we got ready to go on a boat ride and watched the sharks. We got to feed them and I thought that was pretty cool. The next day we went to the Keys of Florida. We drove around to see the sights and we had lunch at a nice restaurant. One of the waitresses asked me if we were rich. I said no, but we had a nice time in Florida.

Untitled
Starlin Fernández, Golden Valley

I love winter in Minnesota, because I do so many things. I like to go skating and snow boarding. In the summertime, I like to go the lakes and go camping. I have so much fun in Minnesota.

Starlin Fernández is originally from the Dominican Republic.

Trip to Arizona
DeShun Langley, Woodbury

When I was in Arizona, the weather was very nice, sunny and dry. It only rained one day. It was hot. I had to get my windows darker in my car. The scenery was nice, and they had houses built into a hill. One Friday night, I went out to Scottsdale to hang out. It was about half an hour from my house. I wish I could have stayed longer in Arizona and found a job there.

The Greatest Day of My Life
Maandeeq Osman, Rochester

Hello my name is Manka. I am from Somalia. I came to the United States on September 11, 2001. It was the greatest day in my life. I knew everything will be a new life, but I never thought my life will be harder than other refugees because of my religion. My flight was Cairo to Holland, Holland to New York, New York to Chicago, Chicago to Tucson, Arizona. People stared at me, but then I didn't know why they stared at me. Now I realize it was my scarf; immediately everyone knew I was Muslim, and they didn't want to trust me.

One day my neighbor and I went to English class. My neighbor was not wearing her scarf, but I was. We were riding the city bus to school when this guy got on the bus. He sat down across from me and said, "F you B. Do you speak?" I didn't say anything. He called me many names; he was nasty. Then he spit in my face and said, "B, I think you need to go back to where you came from." I was very scared. I didn't move. I didn't know what to say, but what made me worried and sad was nobody said anything. A couple guys were laughing. I felt this was my last day ever on this earth. When the bus stopped, this guy got off like he didn't do anything wrong. When I reached my last destination, I wanted to get off the bus, but I couldn't move, nor could I talk.

I told my teacher and shared with the students. Everyone said that is sad and be careful. I am very thankful that he didn't kill me, and I am grateful for the experience. I know I have to be careful. My teacher and my classmates helped me and stood up for me because I was crying, sad and numb.

Whatever happened that day made me a very strong person. I don't want to sit and feel sorry for myself. I am strong. I am thankful for my teacher, my family and my friend, also those who didn't feel sorry for me, but said it's okay if you want to cry, we will listen to you. I came a long way; I am a very happy, healthy person and I forgave him. I am still happy to be in the United States and have a better life and peace.

Maandeeq Osman is originally from Somalia.

Funny Story
Jua Chang, Minneapolis

I remember the first time my wife and I went to the Bangkok International Airport to come to the United States. I was confused at that time, because we walked and walked in the airport. I didn't know which way was the way to inside the airplane.

When we arrived at New York City, my wife was hungry so she wanted to eat something. Then I didn't know how to say and speak English, because I never learned before, but I tried to use my idea to go find some foods for my wife.

Then I walked and looked around anywhere until I saw a lot of foods. That food made me feel very happy. I thought I'll get some foods for my wife. Then, after that I watched the people buy food some people talked a lot but some people had nothing to say. They made a line and chose the foods they wanted and then paid money for the foods. So I did the same that they did and I should go take the foods I want and I pay money for them, but they talked a lot to me and I didn't know and understand what they said. I just smiled.

At the end, I found the foods for my wife and I saw my wife was happy, and I was happy too.

Jua Chang is 25 years old and is originally from Thailand.

My Experience
Christina Hae, Saint Paul

When I first came to the U.S., I felt very bad because I didn't understand English. When I took the airplane, I had air sickness. I thought I would die. I was very dizzy. The airplane had a little problem, but they fixed it. So, we came late. We had to take another airplane, but we didn't have any more time. We had just five minutes before the next airplane would fly. So we had to run quickly. I had no appetite, and I was very tired. I didn't want anything in the airplane for three days. I didn't like to eat their food, because I had never eaten that food before. So, I felt so bad, but I was also so excited about seeing a different place with different buildings and different seasons.

What Will Happen If You Get Crazy About Something?
Abdirisak Asad, Minneapolis

Hi. I would like to tell a story about a man who loved soccer. One night he was sleeping and he started dreaming that he was playing soccer. While he was sleeping in bed, he had a dream that he was kicking a ball but instead he kicked the foot of his bed. When he woke up his foot was broken. I felt sorry for him, so let this be a lesson. Please don't be so crazy about something.

Abdirisak Asad is originally from Somalia East Africa.

New to the Country
Amina Sahal, Minneapolis

I came to the United States in 1999. I came to San Diego, California. I came with some of my family. When I got off the plane, I was looking for snow. Unfortunately, I didn't see it. I was so disappointed when I didn't see snow. I was talking to myself and said, "This is not the United States." At the same time, I saw a sign which had a big screen and showed everything. After that I said, "This is America, but something is not right. When I was in Africa I heard that America has a lot of snow, especially at the end of the year." After a few minutes, we went home. Before we got home, I opened the car window and looked for snow. I saw nothing. When we got home and everybody else was busy with other things, I was the only person who was interested to see snow. Around 10 p.m., everybody went to bed to sleep except me. I didn't sleep all night because I thought I could see snow. At 7 a.m., everybody woke up. A friend of mine said, "Didn't you see snow?" I said, "No, I didn't see it." She told me this state doesn't have snow. I asked her which state has snow. She said, "Minnesota has a lot of snow." After a few months I decided to come to Minnesota. I saw snow. I was so happy, excited and overcome.

Amina Sahal is originally from Somalia.

Trip to Laos
Anonymous, Saint Paul

Hi, my name is Houa Vang. I have been in the United States for five years. April 21st, 2009 was my first trip to go back to visit my family in Laos. This was the trip that my husband and I planned for our five-year anniversary. During our journey, we crossed two continents and one ocean. It was a very long flight.

When I got to the airport in Laos, I saw my parents, my brothers, and my sisters. I was so happy and felt very relieved. The weather in Vientiane was very, very hot. We stayed there for two days. Then we decided to go to the village where my parents live. It took about five hours of driving to get there. That village is in the very high mountains, so the temperature there was about 85 degrees in the daytime. It was much better than in the city. When we got to the place where my mom and dad live, they had a very big party for my husband and me. We had lots of relatives and friends come to see us and enjoy the party with us. We had a good time together, and they were so glad to see my husband and me.

We stayed in that village about one week. Then we also went to many cities to see some popular places that tourists like to go visit. We saw a waterfall, the big jars, and other places too. We wanted to go to visit some more cities, but we didn't have enough time, so we went back to Vientiane to wait for the date to come back home. On May 11th, my husband and I had to leave Vientiane. It made me sad and also made me feel tired to think of flying back to America. When the airplane took off and flew up to the sky, I missed my parents so much I cried and cried. My husband wiped my tears from my eyes and said, "Don't cry, we will come back again someday." I felt better after that. I want to tell all of you that travel is a good memory forever.

Bad to Good in the USA
Wah Ka Paw Do Mu, Saint Paul

My name is Wah Ka Paw. I was born on December 22nd, 1975 in Burma, Wah Ka village near the Hay K'load, Measot, Thailand. My country is very beautiful. The river is like a mother and father, always love their kids. The waterfall sound is like music. In my country, the whole family lives together. But some people are no good to take care of their country. Some people are the government and soldiers.

I'm so sad about some people. I have a beautiful country, but I can't live in Burma a long time, because of many problems. The Burmese soldiers often attacked it.

I came to Thailand in 1984 in Hay K'load. Hay K'load is very near Burma. It is a refugee camp. I lived in the refugee camp for 26 years. When I lived in the camp, there were many problems. We were not free to walk and work or do anything. Afraid and not safe. Everybody was scared some people would come to bother us. Some people in Burma and in Thailand outside the camp have habits like a lion. They came and killed people and shot the people and they burned the camp. The camp place was burned two times. All are down. Everybody escapes themselves. The first year is 1998 and second year is 1999. Many people in the camp have problems. It is really hard to go ahead to life because any things and many things are number zero.

In 1999, all people in the Hay K'load camp moved to the Umpien refugee camp in Thailand. All people are happy to move to a new camp. Many people have problems: very rainy, not enough food, house, no good water, sleep very cold and air blow big, etc. Some Thai soldiers are not good, like a lion when they help people. No safe. No freedom to go outside and take daily work. The people are like animals in the bad zoo, many problems.

In 2009, I moved to the USA, the state of Minnesota. I'm married and I study English, math and computer at HAP. My husband and I have one daughter and one son. I live in an apartment, very safe, warm, enough food, not scary, freedom, healthy. I feel that is very good. I hope in my future everything really comes to very good, not bad.

I remember all people in the refugee camp and my new friend, Haw Oo. I lost my country. Now I have a new, good, free country. We all have equal rights.

I pray always may God bless you, good luck in everything.

My Odd Journey
Mustafa Mussa, Minneapolis

My odd journey began when I came from Nairobi, Kenya (in east Africa) to the United States. When the plane was coming in to land at JFK International Airport in New York, I looked down and the land was all white. I thought it was a cloud. After the plane landed, I realized it was not a cloud, it was snow. I didn't know anything about snow or the winter season. I didn't even know about how the weather had different seasons.

A few hours later, I took another airplane around dusk and then I arrived in the Twin Cities around nine o'clock p.m. I met my family and friends, who were waiting for me at the airport. We gave each other huge hugs.

When I finally came out of the airport, it was very cold and slippery. I felt freezing cold—it was my worst day because I didn't bring a jacket with me. I was wearing only a regular shirt. That is why it was the worst day for me.

Three months later, spring was coming. The snow melted. The grass became green and the trees grew leaves. I got another surprise—people stopped wearing their jackets. I was feeling good then. After two more months, I heard something. My brother said it was a tornado warning. That was my third surprise.

Then, after one more month, it was summer and I felt very hot. I was sweating during the day and during the night too. It was very difficult for me to adapt to Minnesota weather.

A Trip to Egypt
Iliana H., Wyoming

I would like to visit Egypt, because I think it is a good place to explore and learn about history. I would like to learn about Egyptian culture. I would also like to see the Nile River, because in the movie *Prince of Egypt*, I saw how the river turned red. I would like to see the pyramids. Maybe one day, when I win the lottery, I will pay for my trip and go to Egypt. If it does not happen that way, I will keep it in my heart and travel there in my next life.

When I Came to the U.S.
Daring E. Martínez-Meza, Minneapolis

Hi. My name is Daring, and when I was sixteen years old, my mom asked me if I would come to the U.S. I was surprised, because I never imagined coming to the U.S. So my mom kept saying that but I never kept that on my mind so I left that. When I turned eighteen, the opportunity was right. My uncle tried to come here, but he lost the way so he just had a few days to get to Guatemala and then take the way for the U.S. But he couldn't get it, so my mom told me you have to go. I couldn't imagine how the U.S. was, so I got on the train and went cruising across Mexico. I felt bad when I left my family. When I came here, everything was different: the house, the cars, the park. So I felt surprised, because everything was new for me. Everybody spoke differently, and I couldn't understand anything. My life in the U.S. was like a start over, was like a new life, was like I'm alive for the second time, like a new opportunity.

Daring E. Martínez-Meza is originally from Guatemala.

Trip to Mexico City
Gabin Gitangwa, Saint Cloud

Last July, I traveled in Mexico with all my family coming from Sao Paulo, Brazil. We were there for holidays. We chose this city, because it's one of the cities in the world most visited, and we needed to see in person this city, the people who live there, how the economy is organized, and what were the principal activities.

On July 29th, 2009, we took Mexico Airlines flying to Mexico. It was a long trip, almost eleven hours. We left Sao Paulo at 10 p.m., and we arrived in Mexico City at 9 a.m. When we arrived at the airport, we took the taxi to go to the hotel. We were very frustrated, because we didn't have confidence in the driver. He looked very bad.

Our thinking was to get in very quickly to the hotel. When we arrived at the hotel, we had a big problem with the communication. We speak French and Portuguese. In Mexico, they speak Spanish. In the hotel, no one spoke any of our languages. It was funny. Since we had our reservation, we were through in our room. We took baths, got dressed, and went out to look for lunch.

I already knew about Mexican food, because one of my friends traveled before me to Mexico City. He had many problems eating well. The big difficulty was all foods had a lot of pepper. My son has a big problem eating. He didn't like any food. He passed many times without eating something. We bought only yogurt for him. He lost a lot of weight. But I think it was a good experience to discover how other people live.

The day after, we were out to visit a city. Mexico City is a big city but very dangerous. Before going out in the reception, they told us to be careful. They have many gangsters there. We were afraid and frustrated with this news. The city is beautiful and sunny, but it has a lot of people there and a lot of traffic. We visited a subway. It was awful to move in the subway, because it was old and had many people inside and no security.

When we were moved, all people were looking at us, because we are black. They don't have black people there. It was very strange for us.

The trip was hard for us, but a good experience. We liked it. We ask other people to try the same experience like we did.

Gabin Gitangwa is originally from the Democratic Republic of Congo.

Christmas Day
Long Nguyen, Saint Cloud

Christmas is the good time to be with family and celebrate. This Christmas was very special for the Vietnamese community, because it was at the Hinkley Casino.
They have a special Christmas day for the Vietnamese. They have a seafood buffet and a Vietnamese concert.

We planned to go there for entertainment. All my family went there in three cars. The weather looked nice and the road okay to drive there. We got there right in time to eat and enjoy the concert. After the concert, we were ready to go home. I picked up my car and waited for my brother and my cousin to drive home together. When we got out of the casino, there was snow already. I told my brother and my cousin to drive slowly to go home, because the road was very slippery. I let them go first and I went after them. The road was really bad and with a lot of snow and ice underneath the snow.

We drove slowly to go home, and we were okay and we were almost to Foley. Suddenly, my cousin's car lost control and went to the other side of the road and went into the ditch.

We were so scared, because my mom and my brother were in my cousin's car.

Luckily, there were no other cars coming in his direction. Then he slid into the ditch and no one got hurt. Luckily, the truck behind us stopped and helped us to call the police and the tow truck. That was nice and very kind of him to help us out. We sat in the car for thirty minutes until the policemen and the tow truck came and pulled my cousin's car out of the ditch. His car was okay. It had just a little damage in the front, but he could drive home after that.

That was a scary experience of driving in the snow, and I will never go or drive somewhere in bad conditions again.

Long Nguyen is 36 years old and is originally from Vietnam.

A Place to Visit
Tim Hubble, Oakdale

I want to see Hawaii because of Pearl Harbor. During its history we lost lots of men and women in our Armed Forces. We lost lots of civilians and lots of planes. We lost battleships and destroyers. I want to see monuments from World War II.

I am interested in Pearl Harbor because I saw lots of movies about it. My favorite was *Tora Tora Tora*. It showed how American ships were attacked. I would like to see Pearl Harbor before I die.

Fishing Is My Favorite
Anonymous, Saint Paul

Fishing is my favorite habit, so I go fishing almost every weekend. I will go fishing when I don't have school or when I am not busy. I am really crazy about fishing, so that's why I go fishing a lot. Most of the time, I will go fishing by myself, but sometimes I go fishing with my brother-in-law and his sons. They are crazy about fishing like me, so that's why we can go fishing together. Every time when we go fishing, we will go by my car. I am the person who fishes for my family now because my parents are too old for going fishing. My wife likes fishing, but she isn't able to because she has to take care of our kids when I am not at home with them. We have lived in the United States for more than four years, but she has gone to fish only a few times. She isn't crazy about fishing like me, but she does like fishing. Fishing is one kind of exercise that people usually do for exercise. I don't really care about eating fish, but my kids do. Every time I catch fish and bring them home, my kids will be happy because they know they are going to have fish for their meals. I am the person who cooks fish for my family. I know how to cook fish better than other people who live in my family.

I will tell you about my fish cooking. First, I prepare a fresh fish that's ready to cook. Then, I will pour some oil into a pan and put the pan on the stove. I will heat the oil until it's hot, and then put the fish into the pan with the hot oil. And you fry the fish until it's cooked. Then you can eat it with your family. I forgot to tell you one thing that I like about fish. I would say I like fried fish. Every time when I have my meals, I will have a fried fish.

My First Time to the United States
Dung Nguyen, Minneapolis

In my life, maybe I'll never forget the first trip to the Unites States. When I sat on the plane, I was very anxious. Did you know that I am afraid of traveling by airplane? I saw people sleeping deeply, but I couldn't sleep at all. In my head, I only hoped that the airplane landed safely, so that I could see my husband and his family. It took me twenty hours from Vietnam to Minneapolis. In the end, the airplane landed on time. The first sentence I said was "Thank God because God protected me." Finishing my documents in the USA airport, I was in a hurry to bring my luggage to the gate where my husband and the family were waiting for me. When they saw me, they were very happy, especially my husband. We took many photographs together to have memories of my first arrival in the United States.

When the door at the airport opened, we went to my husband's car. Oh, I felt very cold. I never had this feeling of cold when I was in Vietnam, because Vietnam is a tropical country. My country has two seasons—dry season and rainy season. One thing surprised me; that is snow. I had never seen snow with my own eyes. I only saw snow through television. It's very nice. At that time, I thought it was very romantic for my husband and me to walk in the falling snow.

Dung Nguyen is originally from Vietnam.

The Grapes

Last month, I harvested the grapes in a nice winery up a mountain. The name of the grape was "white zibibbo," but actually the color was gold. They were bright under the sun. They were very ripe, and when I grabbed them in my hand, I found out they were heavy and sticky. The taste was so sweet it was like putting sugar in my mouth.

I am Cinzia Pucciani, an over-40-year-old Italian lady. I moved to the USA with my husband a few years ago. My hometown is named Pietrasanta (holystone), an artistic and multicultural place in between the mountains and the Mediterranean Sea. I have a nursing background. I love people and solitude with the same intensity. The contact with nature makes me feel regenerated (I visited all Minnesota State Parks), and to stay with children brings me joy. I have a calm, creative, intuitive, and thoughtful personality. I am always learning from the world; sometimes I have to lower my expectations and sometimes life gives to me unexpected beautiful things. I live in Cold Spring and my main goal is to extend my family.

Planning Our First Family Trip to Cameroon
Anonymous, Forest Lake

I would like to visit Cameroon, because it's the country where my husband was born. I want my sons to know where their father was born and grew up. They will learn about the culture and how life is different between the USA and Cameroon. I would love for my sons to meet the family in Cameroon and see how they live. Then they would value and appreciate what they have. I want them to know how fortunate we are living in this wonderful country.

Something I'm thinking about our travel to Cameroon is the long trip. It is about twenty hours to go to Bamenda, the city of my husband's family. I don't know how uncomfortable it is traveling with kids, and also I'm pregnant. I don't know if I need to wait until after the little baby comes or go before the baby is born. I wonder how my kids would deal with the long trip. I'm thinking to ask friends how they managed their kids in the airplane and what I could do to make the kids have fun on the way. Anyway, I would love to go, no matter what.

My Journey
Davone Chanthavongsa, Elk River

I was too young to understand the significance of what my father would tell me; he passed away last year on August 24, 2009. Even though he is no longer with me, his words will remain in my heart forever and I would like to share them with you.

The sun was begging to set over our tiny village in Bhan Dong Muang, Laos. You will not find it on a map because it is located deep in the jungle. My father was a prominent man in our country. However, he sold most of our family's belongings to take a trip that would literally change my whole world.

We could only take what we could carry on our backs because our journey would be a long path. My grandmother carried me, my mother held my older sister, and my brothers and my father took what we needed to survive on our trip. We were escaping Laos and leaving behind communism, poverty, and hardship, all in exchange for a chance at the land of opportunity.

We traveled by boat down the Mekong River at night trying to find a refugee camp in Thailand. The evening was very calm. My father sat at the end of the boat, never taking a second to even blink. Our guide blindly took us through dangerous waters. At any moment, if we were spotted, soldiers would have killed us all on the spot.

They gave my sister and me sleep medicine so we wouldn't make any noises. I was on my grandmother's lap. I don't remember much from my early childhood but I will forever remember the expression on her face when I woke up. The moon lit her pale face. She looked so strong, but her stare was as blank as the night air. When she saw that my eyes were opened, in a hushed roar, she silently screamed "Ow ya mah," meaning grab the medicine!

All the tension startled me, but before I opened my mouth to scream, my father hovered over me and put his firm hand over my mouth to muffle my cry. I felt this horrendous liquid being lodged down my throat and my body became instantly numb. I woke up the next day to a very busy place. We made it to the camp. Our journey would eventually have a destination. We were on our way to America!

Coming to the United States
Eliud Velázquez, Rochester

Moving from Mexico to the United States, I was looking for better opportunities, safety, and education for my children. I had a desire to come to the United States. It was hard for my husband and for me, too. Our children were small, so we didn't ask them if they wanted to move. After we were thinking about moving, we desired to do that. My husband came first to get a job, and my children and I stayed in Mexico while he made some money. When he left from Mexico, it was sad for us, because we did not know when we would be together again. I always prayed to God to be with him again, and my children wanted to see their dad too.

After four or five months, my husband called me, and he was ready to bring us to the United States. I was scared because I didn't know what will happen with us in this country. We didn't know the language, and we didn't have much family and friends. So we arrived in the United States. Our lives have changed completely since then. At first, it was very difficult to get accustomed to new things. The new language and everything was different for us, but we felt more safety, and my children will have better opportunities and better education.

Now we have been living in this country for twelve years, and I hope my children appreciate all the good opportunities they have in their lives. I miss my country a lot, but I give thanks to God for giving me all the things He has given to my family and to me too.

Eliud Velázquez is originally from Mexico.

Happy, but Dog Tired
VG, Saint Paul

Most of us have a pretty regular lifestyle. With that said, the same applies to me. I have everyday work where I spend part of my day and a home where memories are made. However, besides these things, there is one I love the most. The special but short time of the year I am going to talk about is vacation.

Different people have different thoughts on how to spend their vacation—make it more memorable and have a rest at the same time. However, before we move on, I would like to say that I am a big fan of active vacations. Lying on a beach, having a soda, and doing nothing is a story of someone else rather than me.

Last year, my family, friends and I went down to South Dakota to do some hiking and outdoor photography. There were different places to see including caves, ghost towns, and, my favorite, Mount Rushmore.

If you are willing to have the most memorable vacation, then pack your staff and go down to South Dakota. But keep in mind, getting dog tired is a way to an active vacation.

VG is originally from Estonia.

The Best Vacation
Keith Kinning, Maplewood

Every summer, during the month of August, for two weeks, as a family we would pack up the minivan and travel to different states. One of the road trips was to the Canadian Rockies National Park called Banff. As we were driving through North Dakota, the kids were getting a little restless, so we stopped at a town called Minot. They had a state fair going on and had interesting displays of different kinds of animals. As we left Minot, North Dakota, we headed for Canada and the city called Calgary. In Calgary, they have a display of an Indian village. Then we drove a short way to Banff National Park. The mountains and lakes are beautiful. Perhaps the mountains certainly can hold a mysterious power over the imagination. One of the lakes that really stood out was Lake Louise. Lake Louise stood out because it was early in the morning, and the lake was so still you could see the reflection of the mountain in the lake. It was a long drive for the family, but after seeing the lakes and mountains it was worth it.

New Arrival
Abdulkadir Mursal, Minneapolis

I arrived in the United States of America on March 29th, 2000. My family and I were on board a Northwest Airline plane. The pilot of the airplane announced that the airplane will land at JFK Airport soon. All the people on board cheered joyfully. A few minutes after the pilot's announcement, I heard and felt the landing of the airplane as it ran onto the runway. When the people started to stand I could not do the same because my legs had jet lag weakness. Finally I stood and walked into the aisle of the airplane. It was the end of a long journey by plane from Kenya to the United States of America. It took sixteen hours of airplanes and six hours of transit in Amsterdam, the Netherlands. Eventually we got off the airplane and into the JFK airport. We had a sign from the International Immigration Organization. As soon as we got off the plane, the IMA employee was waiting for us and led us into the customs office.

We stood in a long line and got our papers stamped according to the refugee law. I led my family because I was the only one in my family who spoke English. In late evening, we were transported from the airport terminal into New York City refugee transit hub staffed by new refugees who hailed from Eastern Europe and Balkan areas. The center entertained us that night. The food was rice and chicken. About midnight my brother woke up and prayed the dawn prayer according to the watch he had, which was eight hours ahead of local time.

Abdulkadir Mursal is originally from Somalia.

Boundary Waters Canoe Area
Ahmed Hassan, Columbia Heights

How fun it was to be at the Boundary Waters Canoe Area. That was the best time of my life. In 2002, I was in the program that took us to Duluth and then went north to get canoes. We spent the night in the tents. Then in the morning, we traveled until lunchtime. At lunchtime, we took our break. Afterwards, we moved on to the next stop. The second night, we all came together to introduce ourselves. Finally, in the morning we headed home. That was how much fun I had at the Boundary Waters Canoe Area.

Luck of the Opal
Anonymous, Minnetonka

Some people say that the Opal can be an unlucky stone. I'm here to tell you that it is not true in my experience.

I went on a vacation with my friend to Mexico. First, we stopped at Taxco. It's a small silver mining city. I bought an Opal ring. It wasn't an expensive one, but I liked it a lot.

A couple days later, we went from Taxco to Acapulco. It was a hot and gorgeous day and we headed to the beach. On the way to the beach, I met a nine-year-old Mexican girl. I don't speak Spanish and she didn't speak

English, but somehow we liked each other. After awhile, my friend and I went swimming. Suddenly, my beautiful Opal ring slipped off my finger. I lost my ring in the ocean. We tried looking in the bottom of the ocean to find my ring. We couldn't find it. Waves were kicking the sand constantly. As far as I could see, there was no way I could recover my ring. I lost my hope. About twenty minutes later, I saw that nine-year-old girl again. I tried to tell her that I lost my ring in the ocean. About five minutes later, she was calling me and waved at me to come over. She found my ring.

Years later, I bought a small Black Opal. I had it custom designed into a pendant. My sister-in-law visited from Seattle. We went to the North Shore. We stopped at a rock shop to look for Agates and looked at more souvenir shops. After awhile, I realized that I lost my Opal necklace. We retraced everywhere we went to. My vacation was ruined. We came home with a heartache. After we came home, we put an ad in their local newspaper. About two weeks later, someone called me. They had my pendant. What a nice person! She told me that once she had lost her gold chain which made her see how I felt.

So, as you can see, Opal is a very lucky stone for me.

My Life in the United States
Jorge L., Minneapolis

I came in March of 1999. My mom had been here for three years. For me, it was a surprise to see the snow, because in Ecuador there is no snow. I had three weeks at home with nothing to do, because my mom was working two jobs, and after that I began to go to school. I knew friends in the church and with them, I went to meetings, holidays, dinners, etc.

Two months later, I went with my mom to Chicago to see my aunt and bring her here to Minnesota during the summer. After that, I went again to school for some months.

My sister came the next year, and we moved to New Brighton. In July 2000, I went to California to an event named *Encuentro 2000*. There were a lot people, but it was something pretty. I visited other states: New York, Florida, Georgia and Washington. When I started to work, my jobs were always in restaurants. Right now, I am married and happy with my wife.

Looking Back
Nan Xiao, Saint Paul

Last August, I came to the Unites States. It was the first long trip of my life, and it will be my best memory. I left from Shanghai and changed planes in Tokyo. After that, I changed to another plane in Los Angeles. Finally, I arrived in my target city, Minneapolis.

It was a very long trip! Maybe it took about fifteen hours. Many friends told me that it is so boring on the plane, but I didn't think so. Because I bought my ticket too late, they didn't have any seat for me in my wife's plane. I had to go by plane to the United States by myself. It was so difficult for me, because my English was so poor. I had to fill the I-94 form by myself. I didn't know anything about this and nobody could help me. The airplane personnel were American or Japanese. No one could speak Chinese. "Oh, no, maybe I can't get to the United States if I have any mistakes on this form," I thought. When I filled in the blank for sex, I thought, "that's so easy, I can do it." So I didn't think carefully and filled "man" in the blank. But then I felt maybe "male" was better. I checked it in the dictionary. I found I had made a mistake. Oh no, what could I do? I had to ask for another I-94 form. I was afraid the airline personnel were laughing at me. I felt foolish! But I must do that! The stewardess was so kind. She gave me a new form and told me, "It doesn't matter." At that time, I was really grateful to her. She looked like an angel. I was very careful filling out the new form. It was correct this time.

I arrived in Los Angeles. I needed to change planes to get to Minneapolis. When I passed through airport security, it was a little different from China. I saw everyone took off their shoes and belts. So, I took them off, too. You know, in China, we didn't need to take them off. I just did everything like the person who was in front of me. Thank goodness, I passed security.

At last, I arrived at the airport in Minneapolis, my target city. I met my wife and her friends. Then I relaxed. They asked me, "How was your trip?" I said, "It was a very special experience! I loved it!"

Nan Xiao is 28 years old and is originally from China.

Jayson Knutson, Bemidji

My First Time Traveling to the USA
Akoua Ofridam, Minneapolis

I left Togo on October 30, 2004. I went from Togo to France. When I transferred airplanes, I had six hours to spend in France. I didn't know what to do. It was my first time in France. I didn't go anywhere. I was afraid of getting lost.

After six hours, I took another airplane to New Jersey. When I arrived in New Jersey, the man who was supposed to pick me up was coming, but he didn't want to let me know he was the one. By surprise, I went to him and asked him if he was from Togo and he said yes. This time he asked me if I had money to take a taxi to New York. I said yes, and I got in a taxi. The man followed the taxi because he directed the taxi driver. When I arrived in New York, the driver said to pay ninety dollars!

After two days, my cousin's wife's sister came to ask why I brought my son with me. She said that she looked for a job for me, but I wasn't bringing my son. She wanted to send my husband to Alabama for a job. She didn't even ask me if I had started my Social Security paperwork, so I called my cousin Kodzo who lived in Minneapolis and told him I wanted to go to Washington D.C. Then my cousin said, "I'm here, don't worry, come here." That's why I'm in Minneapolis now.

Akoua Ofridam is 44 years old and is originally from Togo.

Travel
Anonymous, Hopkins

I made plans for my life to visit different countries, starting from Quetzaltenango, Guatemala for two months in January 2001. Then I came to the USA, Brooklyn, New York in April 2002. I was single, so it was an

Travel and Adventure - 131

adventure. I noticed there were more cities I should visit, so I went to Chicago, Las Vegas, Colorado and Minnesota.

I went back to Mexico in 2008 for vacation. It was so different; it was weird. Mexico has beautiful places to live and different types of weather. No one controls you. You feel so good going anywhere, anytime you want, without telling or asking anybody. Now I'm planning to go back to Mexico in 2011 and stay at least six months and then move to Canada to visit new cities and learn a new culture.

My Journey
Remeriza Laurie, New Brighton

I have moved to the United States and have lived here about eight years. I have a family and had a wonderful child. When I first came in this country, it was hard to adapt to their culture, weather and especially to their own way of education. Unfortunately, it was the same form of education that we have but it's just a different way of education level process. Living in this country, it's a lot different in the way in their standard of living compared to our country. It was a good education and a good experience being able to work with many other cultures. It's a good accomplishment to become an American citizen. I was looking forward to fulfilling for my next goal pursuing a new career and taking an Accounting class to be able to develop my passion based upon my good experience and interest. I'm looking forward to committing my goal for the near future.

Remeriza Laurie is 33 years old and is originally from the Philippines.

(Excerpt)
German Lema, Minneapolis

As a kid growing up in a foreign country, I never dreamed about enlisting in the U.S. Navy. These thoughts are not in most of kids' minds.

My dad brought me to this great nation when I was a teen. I struggled for the first few years in school. Schoolmates would make fun of and laugh at me, because I did not understand the language.

As a student in high school, I used to see recruiters from the Armed Forces come and go. One day, it caught my attention. I became more interested in joining the Navy.

During my senior year, I decided to start the process and move forward with the paperwork. Before signing the contract, I went cold turkey; I determined I was too young.

A few years later, after I was married, I again decided to join. This time, there was no turning back. I walked into a recruitment office and started the paperwork process. Navy and Marines recruiting offices were next to each other. The Marine recruiter almost convinced me to join the Marines, but in my mind, there was only room for Navy.

Leaving for boot camp was nerve racking. I almost did an about-face when I arrived at the airport in Chicago.

German Lema is originally from Ecuador.

ONLY 40 POUNDS

I came to Minnesota on July 6th, 2008. I could only bring one suitcase, weighing 40 pounds. What could I bring that only weighed up to 40 pounds?

I was thinking and thinking; the choice was very difficult. I tried to put a value on all the things I owned, and finally, I wanted to keep them all. I loved my wedding pictures, my wood furniture, my old computer, my big mirror, my sewing machine, my little radio...all my things that made me feel at home. But I could only carry 40 pounds, including the weight of the suitcase. I closed my eyes and my heart, and I sold all the stuff I had. I felt really sad.

I heard it was cold in Minnesota, so I packed only some warm clothes for the Minnesota winter, shoes, some pictures, a rosary, a Bible, some gifts from my friends and an English/Spanish dictionary.

Soon I realized that the most important things that I can carry are myself—my memories, my culture, my faith and all that is in me. My family (my dear husband and my lovely son) and I started this adventure in the USA together. Material things come and go, but the love you carry in your heart can go with you everywhere.

Martha Carbajal is an ESL student in Rosemount-Apple Valley-Eagan ABE. She is 42 years old and lives in Eagan with her husband and ten year old son. She was born in Mexico where she made homemade salsa for distribution through shops. She came to Minnesota in 2008 with her family when her husband changed his work. In her free time, Martha likes to swim, read, and study English in her class. She hopes someday to run a salsa business again.

Travel and Adventure - 133

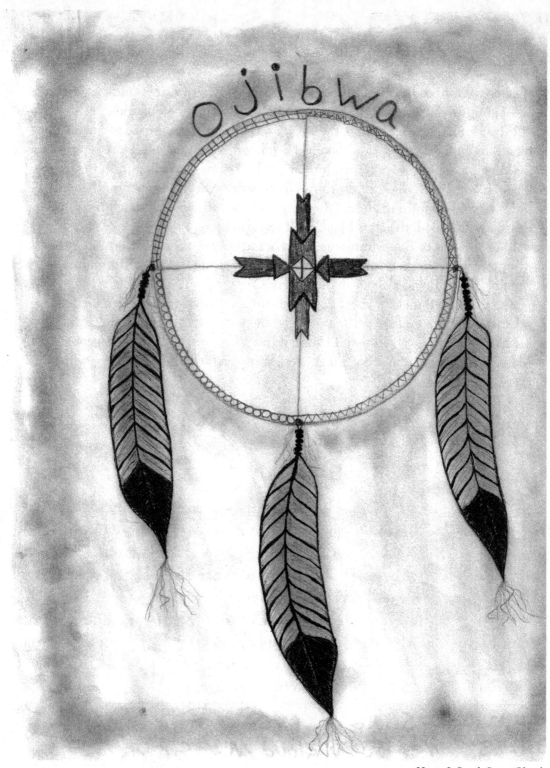

Kevin L Sund, Saint Cloud

Celebration and Tradition

Good Story
Qali Haji, Minneapolis

A long time ago, there was a king. His name was Cawale. He had two boys and three girls—Farah and Abdi, Lul, Asha, and Halimo. His wife's name was Sahro. One day, a poor man named Jama came to the king's door and knocked. The guard opened the door and asked why he knocked at the door. The poor man said, "I want the king's girl." The guard said, "Do you know the king's girl?" The poor man said, "I don't know, but I dreamed several times I was married to her. She birthed two boys and three girls." The guard said, "Do you want me to send you to jail or kill you? Are you mad?" The poor man said, "No, but I want to tell my request to the king." The guard shut the door and said, "You are a foolish man."

The poor man knocked at the door another time. The king heard the sound of the knock and said, "Who is knocking at the door?" The guard said, "A poor man." The king said, "Please give him food." The guard said, "He does not want food." "What does he want?" The guard said, "He wants one of your daughters." The king was angry and said, "Send him to jail, please." One of his boys, Farah, said, "Please, my father don't send him to jail. If you send him to jail, Allah will be angry with you and you will die soon, because Allah doesn't allow us to jail people without reason."

Then the king thought and at last got a decision. "Give him new clothes and a bath and send him to me." When the poor man did this, he came and stood in front of the king. Then the king asked the name of the girl he wanted. The poor man said, "Asha." Then the king gave her to him in marriage and said to the poor man, "Today you are family." He gave him much money, and so the poor man became a rich man.

Qali Haji is originally from Somalia.

The Story of Animals
Maliya Aliy, Minneapolis

There is a story from my beautiful country of Oromiya. There are big mountains with different names in my blessed country. There is a pretty forest and lots of different animals in the forest such as lion, ox, zebra, hyena, baboon, gorilla, monkey, etc. They had a leader and vice president. The leader was Lion; the vice president was Ox. They were best friends. One day they were walking in the forest. Mother Hyena gave birth to a litter. One was very pretty. Mother Hyena loved the litter. Lion and Ox saw Hyena's litter. They said, "Wow, they're very cute!" Ox said, "It's my litter! Can you take it from Hyena for me?" "Yes, why not? You like it, Ox?" "Yes!" Lion said, "Ok I can do that." Hyena heard that and she cried. All the animals were amazed. Then the leader called all of them for a meeting to decide who got to keep this litter.

All of them came on time except Rat. She was making the hole for home. When she was done she came late, saying "Dear President, I am very sorry I came late," and smiled. Lion said, "That's OK. By the way, can you come on time next time?" She said, "I will try my best." Lion said, "Hmm. Are you kidding me? I am the leader! What happened to you?" Rat said, "The forest floor was broken and I sewed it, so I'm late." "Do you hear that, everyone?" said Lion. "The forest floor was broken." They said, "No," because they are scared of him. Rat said, "Everyone, do you hear that an ox had a hyena baby?" And she laughed at Lion. The leader got mad and ran to catch Rat. Rat already had made a hole for a home. She just ran around in front of his face laughing at him. The leader was angry. He shouted, cried and said, "Everyone, make a circle to catch her, then give her to me! I will show her who I am!" Then they made a circle to catch her. And she said, "Everyone, make a circle to dance!" And she got into her hole. The leader and Ox felt shame, and the leader said to Ox, "Oh my friend, please get out of my face! You make me feel shame." And Ox and Lion separated. Hyena was happy to keep her baby!

What I Miss
Toan Ly, Apple Valley

I come from Vietnam. I have been living in Minnesota for two years. I still remember the first day when I got here. That was in winter and I got a cold. I was sick for a whole week. It was terrible for me.

I really like my life here now because it's not too hard to find a job, and the pay from my work is not bad. In my country, it is not easy to find a job and most of the jobs get very low pay. That's why I moved to Minnesota.

The one thing I miss in my country is the Lunar New Year. We usually take a week off for that. It is fun. There are people doing the dancing lion in the park. We all dress up, go visit friends and relatives, and drink and eat. It is a wonderful holiday!

Toan Ly is originally from Vietnam.

How To Find Happiness
Anonymous, Mounds View

A lot of people want to be happy, but they can't. Some people think that money brings happiness. Some people think when you change your life, you will be happy. Some people know that happiness comes from inside, but they can't find it.

My mom told me a story about an old man who lived in a small village. This man caught one fish each day and was happy. The king of the country was lost, and he met this old man. The king saw that the old man was happy and he was surprised. The king asked him, "Why are you happy? You have no money, no wife, no house and no family. I have everything but I am not happy."

The old man told him, "It is because you are greedy."

The king told the old man, "If I give you a boat you can catch many fish."

The old man said, "So what?"

The king said, "Sell the fish and make money."

The old man said, "So what?"

The king said, "You will be happier with money."

The old man said, "But I am already happy."

The king realized that happiness comes from inside.

A Happy Memory
Khadra Askar, Minneapolis

When I was young, the happiest time for me was the holiday. Usually kids are happy most of the time. All they think about is play, how many friends they play with today and how many games they play, not like adults. For me one day the holiday Eid was coming and my father was away. He traveled one time a year. Then I asked my mom and my brother, "Tomorrow will be Eid. Do you think Daddy will come?" Then I went to bed. My father came at midnight while we were sleeping. So in the morning I heard my father talking. Then I went to him to say "Hello father," and he told me he bought Eid clothes for me. It was a beautiful dress, and I was so happy. All the kids played and the food was nice. All the family was there. It was a happy time.

White Snow, White Christmas
María Mercedes Zumarraga, Hopkins

As a dream that came true, when I first came to the United States of America, I expected to celebrate Christmas in winter, but this winter was different than the winter we usually have in my previous country, Ecuador.

It was awesome, December 24th. I wake up. I open my eyes, and I open the curtains. It is snowing. Outside all is white; the flakes of snow are falling again and again and the snow covers the land. I'm still in bed; it is cozy and warm. It is ten. Then it is 11 a.m. I'm hungry and I have to get up. I need a cup of coffee to start the new day, and I get ready to go out. I think how beautiful, how amazing, nature is.

There is a lot of snow. My nephew pushes me down and we start to play. I enjoy playing; I enjoy the snow; I enjoy life. It still is snowing and we are tired and exhausted.

Time runs out, and everybody is excited, in a hurry to go to church to celebrate the most wonderful day of the year, the birth of Baby Jesus. Listening to Christmas carols is special to me, because I feel the spirit and joy of Christmas. The words are very short, sometimes to describe the many blessings we have everywhere, all the time.

At home, all is happiness, and I am thankful to God that I have seen the white snow and am living the white Christmas.

María Mercedes Zumarraga is originally from Cotopaxi, Ecuador.

Thanksgiving Guest
Mohamed Abukar Ali, Coon Rapids

I would like to invite my sister for the special day of Eid. Why have I chosen my sister? Because we have not seen each other for nineteen years. I miss her so much. I would like to see her and have a big dinner together. My sister is the particular guest I would like to invite for my special day of Eid.

Untitled
Mee Her, Minneapolis

Once upon a time in Laos, there was a family. They were going to their garden to weed. Afterwards, they were hungry, so they told their son Senke to go home first with his brother Jay to help their grandma and grandpa prepare dinner. Senke and Jay walked down the path by the river. As they were walking, Senke saw a mother bear with her baby! The mother was scared that Senke would attack the baby, so she killed Jay. So Senke got very mad at the mother bear. Senke then attacked her. The two of them wrestled and rolled down to the river. Senke and the bear became exhausted. Senke then crossed his legs over the bear's leg. The bear was much larger than

Senke, so Senke was under the bear with his head under the bear's chin. Senke held the bear's head and put a rock in the bear's mouth so she could not bite him. He then put his hand into her mouth and pulled her intestines out until she died. Later he went home very sad because he lost his brother, but he was happy to be alive.

Happy Valentine's Day!
Anna Kim, Blaine

I received the nicest gift from my husband. It happened on the first Valentine's Day right after we got married. It's a story from ten years ago. I was 28 years old and pregnant. I was scared, worried, and frustrated about my married life. My husband was a student, he didn't have a job and we didn't have enough money to live on. On that Valentine's Day, I had to give my husband a ride to school, but he didn't get me anything. I was angry with him. It was Valentine's Day. I didn't expect anything from him. I just wanted a small box of chocolates. When I drove the car, I didn't look at him. When he talked to me, I was very mad at him. But when we arrived at school, he wanted me to open the trunk and... I will never forget that moment. He stood outside holding a bunch of roses, a balloon, a box of chocolates, a big smile on his face, and a lovely Valentine's card. I read the Valentine's card. I just cried. I don't know why. But I remember that moment. My life is always with my husband.

Holidays
Ia Chang, Coon Rapids

When I was a child, we lived in my old country, Laos. We don't have any holidays; we only have New Year's Day. On New Year's Day, everyone wants to have nice clothes and new shoes to wear. There are many kinds of food to eat for New Year's Day. People spend eight to ten days preparing the food. On New Year's Day, girlfriends and boyfriends talk to each other. The mothers and fathers help their son or daughter find a spouse. In my religion, the boyfriend's mom and dad don't like the girlfriend to be lazy. In the USA, the children have freedom to find a husband or wife for themselves.

Ia Chang is originally from Laos.

Love Can Cause Death
Ali Farah, Minneapolis

The first man and woman died for love. They were Bodhari and Hodan. Bodhari was a poor man. He lived in Somalia in Horfadhi city. His parents passed away when he was three years old. He didn't have a family or relatives there. Bodhari grew up without parents. He was nineteen years old. When he was deciding to start a little business he opened a small bakery. So once upon time, Hodan came to his bakery to buy breads. She was a very beautiful girl. She amazed him. He asked her name and she told him her name. He told her his name too. Immediately, Bodhari fell in love.

After months he tried to let her know that he loved her, but unfortunately she refused because he was a poor man. Then he was disappointed about her. Bodhari got depression. The reason Hodan refused him was because she was eighteen years old and her family was rich. That is why she refused him, and Hodan's family refused him too. Bodhari quit his job because he got depressed.

After six months, Bodhari was near death, so he said, "I would like to see Hodan before I die." Then Hodan came to visit him. When she saw him, Hodan was full in love. After three hours Bodhari died. When he died, she cried. Hodan got sick. After one month, she died within his love.

Ali Farah is originally from Somalia.

The Best Day of my Life
Dede Amagli, Minneapolis

The best day of my life was my eighteenth birthday. My parents woke me early in the morning and gave me a lot of advice. They gave me a big party and I had the privilege to invite all my friends. My mother made me a big birthday cake and I was so happy. I'll never forget that day, because it was my first big day of my life.

What Is Mother's Day?
Mahmood Hassan, Fridley

Mother's Day is always a Sunday. It is the second Sunday in May. On this day, people remember their mothers. Many people wear a flower. Its color has a meaning. A colored flower means that a person's mother is still living. A white flower means a person's mother has died. On the second Sunday in May people remember their mother. A colored flower means they love flowers. You can tell from this story that mothers are very special. Mothers are very, very special!

My Story
Joaquín Maldonado, Robbinsdale

Hi my name is Joaquín Maldonado. I would like to write about a tradition in my country. This tradition is based from the Virgin Mary. There was once a family that promised the Virgin something. This thing was to celebrate in her honor every January. This celebration happens on the 24th to the 26th everywhere around my town. The people gather around and decorate the church with pine branches and different kinds of flowers that may come from trees.

On the first night, everyone dresses up in all kinds of costumes. For example, some dress as delis angels. They are called Morros. After the Morros dance, there is another big event. A bull comes into play. A fire bull is made up. Then it goes off. This celebration is very fun. After the bull, the air fires come in. They are almost like fireworks but better. They go off on ropes that connect from the tree to the ground. On the final days, they have horse races, usually in the afternoons only for those days. After that, there are fighting roosters during the Holidays. The people have a big dance in the night. For three nights, recognized singing group bands play in Mexico, so the people who live in the town have fun. We do this to celebrate in honor of the Virgin.

I was born and grew up in this town. I lived there eighteen years. With my mother, I came to the United States a long time ago. Now in my free time, I practice Aztec Dance. I enrolled in dance last year and I still dance for one reason: because I believe in the saint. On January 22nd and 23rd, we celebrated two days in honor of the saint. Different Aztec groups came to dance in church Sagrado Corazon of Jesus in Minneapolis on 3800 Pleasant Avenue South.

Joaquín Maldonado is 42 years old and is originally from Guerrero, Mexico.

A Traditional Wedding
Tao Vue, Robbinsdale

In Thailand, Hmong people usually get married when they are young—for example, seventeen or eighteen years old. They usually fall in love at that age. When they get married, they will have a big party for their wedding at the groom's house and the bride's house too. The groom and the bride will invite their relatives and friends to come join their party. At the party, they have many kinds of food and drinks. They have red curry, green curry, papaya, alcohol, beer, juice, and water, etc. The groom and the bride have to wear the Hmong traditional clothes during the party because that is their culture.

Hmong people have always followed their tradition and culture and still do this today.

Tao Vue is 24 years old and is originally from Thailand.

Weddings in Russia
Inna Leontyev, Coon Rapids

In my country, women usually get married when they are twenty years old and young men when they are twenty-two. Before getting married, they are friends. A man gives flowers to a woman. When he decides to get married, he gives a diamond ring to a woman. A groom's parents, together with the groom, ride to the bride's house. A bride and her parents cook a special dinner for everybody. They have conversations with each other and decide on the wedding's date. On the wedding day, the bride has a beautiful white dress and a pretty veil on her head. A groom is in a black or white suit. The groom's family gives half of the money for the wedding and bride's family gives another half. They invite 200-300 guests for the party. They have good music. The guests, friends and relatives, give presents for the bride and groom. The wedding lasts for five to eight hours. And then, the bride and groom go to a park with their relatives. Here they take many good pictures for memories. The wedding is awesome!

Inna Leontyev is originally from Russia.

New Years When I Was a Child
Adán Gonzales, Saint Paul

When I was eight years old, I liked to play soccer outside with my friends before the New Year arrived. All the time, we played different games together. After that, we talked about our dreams. For instance, what we would like be when we grew up. At the same time, we talked about goals for the future. Those were my memories, but those things happened during the day. At night, my parents called me, because we had to be ready at ten p.m. every New Years. We had to go the church until midnight. After that, we started to celebrate, eating and drinking coffee, and my family talked with each other.

Things I Like
Der Yang, Brooklyn Park

I would like to tell you about what I like. I like a lot of things that make me feel good and comfortable. Things that I like are sewing, the seasons, and flowers.

The first thing that I like is sewing. I like to sew Hmong traditional clothes for my children and grandchildren. I like to sew Hmong traditional clothes, because I want my children to value and learn more about our Hmong culture.

The second thing I like is all the three seasons in Minnesota. I like summer, fall and winter. I like summer, because when it is hot, my family can get together and have fun with some outdoor activities. Those outdoor activities that we do are barbecue and play volleyball. I like the season of fall, because every time I look outside, it is full of sadness. The color of the leaves and the coolness of the wind make me feel so lonely. I don't even understand why I feel that way toward the season of fall. Winter is the last season

I like, because snow makes everything look bright. The snow seems to light up my heart whenever I see it.

The third thing I like is flowers. Looking at flowers always makes me feel happy. I like the white flower because it represents pure hearts and peace. I also like yellow and purple flowers, because those flowers look like a little girl starting to grow up. This is the third thing that I like.

Today, I still like those things like sewing Hmong clothes, watching the three seasons change, and those beautiful flowers. They light up my world every time I look at them. These things I will always love and look forward to them.

Der Yang is 43 years old and is originally from Thailand.

Mother's Day
Rosa Rome, Saint Paul

My memory is about when I was a child and we celebrated Mother's Day. I liked to celebrate Mother's Day, because it was very fun. All students came together to the mothers' houses, and we made special music for our mothers. It was in the morning at 5:00 a.m. In the afternoon, we made a special dance at the school. We saved money all year for Mother's Day. We bought ice cream, watermelon, and other fruit to make a party for our mothers.

Carnival
Luci Magalhaes, Eden Prairie

There is a tradition in my country called "Carnival," ("Carnaval" in Portuguese) which occurs all over the country for three days, 40 days before Easter—although it is a pagan tradition. There are small celebrations in small cities and big celebrations in big cities. The most famous carnival party is in Rio de Janeiro, on a private street called "Sambodromo." You need to pay admission for this carnival.

There are around thirteen groups called Escola de Samba (Samba School). Each group has around 2,500 members. The Samba School is open to the public during the year for rehearsals. The person chooses their school, buys a costume and joins their school for the parade. When that parade passes through the street for an hour, members have to dance and sing the samba music of the group. At the end there is a contest where the most beautiful costume, the best music, and the best float that fits the theme of the music are chosen.

If you don't go to the "Sambodromo," just watch it on TV or go to a club and have fun. Some people just rest and relax these days. The carnival is for rich and poor; everybody is invited.

People from Brazil are always happy and friendly. During carnival time, there are guests from all over the world. They came to Brazil to see and enjoy the big party. Have you ever seen the carnival in Brazil? If not, come and enjoy.

Luci Magalhaes is originally from Brazil.

Birth of the Prophet Mohammad
Al-Azzawi, Coon Rapids

Writing about the birth of the prophet Mohammed is the birthright of all. Mohammad is the light that illuminates the world. This day is a great occasion celebrated by all Muslims in different ways from one country to another.

In Iraq, people wake up early to prepare all the requirements of the ceremony. The first of them is the servers in the mosques clean up and light all the streets and areas where the celebration will be held. Then they start cooking and bring all the drinks and sweets that will be free to all attendees.

People start to come to the celebration centers, singing songs that reflect their love of the great prophet Mohammad. They are glad and sincere. Everyone lights candles which will cover all the streets and listens to the religious advice that encourages them to love each other.

Everyone wants this day not to end, because it is full of love and peace and reverence to God.

Halloween
Houda Hazzaf, Saint Michael

My first trick-or-treating was last year, when my son was one year and two months old. I saw all the houses decorated with pumpkins at the beginning of October and I asked, "Why?"

The answer was that it was Halloween.

What does "Halloween" mean? It's the holiday when kids wear costumes and they go out trick-or-treating (asking for candy). When I took my son, I was surprised—the houses look like scary caves with special music, and a lot of kids were wearing beautiful costumes: princesses, werewolves or clowns. More than that, I love the most polite and kind people I ever saw. They smiled for kids and gave them too much candy. After all that, when I saw my son's eyes full of joy, I decided to celebrate Halloween every year and enjoy this exciting time of year.

Houda Hazzaf is originally from Morocco.

Christmas Memories
Judith, Waite Park

When I think about my childhood, the experience that I remember the most is Christmas. Now things are different for me, but it is special for my kids. When I was little, we used to stay awake until midnight when we could open the presents my mom bought for us. My dad didn't celebrate Christmas, because that's a very sad time for him. When he was seven years old, his parents died during the Christmas period. However, thanks to my mom, I have beautiful memories of Christmas.

New Years
Hijazi, Coon Rapids

My favorite celebration in my country is New Years. I like celebrating New Years, because I like to go downtown. Winter is a wonderful time of the year.

My favorite part of the celebration is the food. I like to make food, because when I see my children and my husband very happy, it makes me happy too. We are meeting, talking, dancing, and eating together. I like taking pictures together, because I like to remember that celebration.

January first, before the celebration, I will go to supermarket because I need to pay for food and a lot of stuff.

Hijazi is originally from Lebanon.

Thanksgiving Guests
Margarita Polyakova, Coon Rapids

Thanksgiving is an important holiday for all of the country of the USA. I think most people celebrate this holiday. Some people invite guests to their houses. It may be relatives, co-workers, or friends. Some prefer to celebrate alone, and some only with their own families. My big wish would be to celebrate this day with my older daughters—Margarita and Zoya, including, of course, other members of my big family.

All my children are endlessly happy when we are gathered together to celebrate holidays. They so love each other, help me with everything, and take care of each other. But now Margarita and Zoya live separately from us—so far—in another country, Russia. But, I hope my wish to celebrate this wonderful holiday, Thanksgiving, with all of my children will be possible somewhere!

A Favorite Place
Arlan Arnold, Elk River

One of my favorite places is the Dunn Brothers Coffee Shop near my home. Whether before work for a quick cup to go or a more relaxing cup later in the day, the arrival is always stimulating.

Opening the door, you are surrounded by the rich aroma of coffee and welcomed by greetings from neighbors and other familiar faces. The menu is also a pleasant puzzle. Deciding from light or dark roast coffees, espresso, latte, or mocha, flavored or even iced coffees, I truly feel like a kid in a candy store. So whether I have a shot of espresso or a double caramel mocha latte with whipped topping, I always wear a smile here, sharing more than just the brew.

When leaving all the wonderful sights, sounds, smells, and taste, with some feeling of fellowship, I already anticipate my next visit to a favorite place.

16 de Septiembre
Nancy Hernández, Eden Prairie

Diez y seis de Septiembre is Mexico's Independence day. It is celebrated all over the country, and it is special this year, since it is the 200th anniversary. Celebrations are going to be held all during the year.

Usually it starts the night before with a ceremony, where local communities gather and dress up for the event. The most common colors are red, green and white, representing the flag, and there are traditional dresses, hats and flags. A ceremony is held by the schools which prepare traditional dances, poetry and plays representing the events as they occurred 200 years ago.

The local authorities choose a girl to be the queen of the event, and she will represent the Spanish people who came to Mexico and dominated for many years. On the other hand, they will have the heroes and personalities dressed as the native Aztecs.

Later, after the show is done, they give "El Grito de Independencia" by the President—he will say "Viva Mexico." The chapel bells will ring, and fireworks will be displayed.

The next morning, the floats that have been decorated with flowers are ready for the big parade. All the people dress up in the traditional Mexican costumes. Horses have a special place since they were brought to Mexico by the Spanish.

When you walk down the main street, the smell of food and the decorations with big flags make you feel at home and proud of your roots.

At the end of the parade, in the downtown, a stage is ready for the main ceremony with live music and dancers. The final number is a reenactment of the fight between the Aztecs and the Spaniards, taking off the crown of the Queen representing the freedom of the Mexican country. They dance and celebrate all together.

This is one of many traditions that Mexico celebrates year after year.

Nancy Hernández is 29 years old and is originally from Mexico.

My Traditions
Maricela Coronado, Rochester

Hello, my name is Maricela. I'm from Mexico and I have two kids: one boy and one girl. My daughter's name is Naydelith, and my son's name is Ariel Alexandro. I am married; my husband is from Mexico too. We have eight years together.

I want to tell you about my traditions in my country. On January 1st, we celebrate the New Year, Año Nuevo. January 6th is Three Magic Kings, Los Tres Reyes Magos.

On February 2nd, we celebrate the blessed virgin of San Juan, La Virgin de San Juan. On February 5th is celebration of Constitution Day, Dia de la Constitucion. February 22nd is God Cristo, Dia de Dios Jesucristo. February 24th is Mexico Flag, Dia de la bordera de Mexico.

On March 7th a big party at my town is La Fiesta en mi Pueblo. April 30th is Kid Day, Dia del Niño. May 1st is Day of the Work, Dia del Trabajo. May 10th is Mother's Day, Dia de las Madres. June 18th is Father's Day, Dia de los Papás. On June 28th all schools take vacations, Todas las Escuelas Toman Vaccaciones.

On September 15th, we celebrate Independence Day, Dia de la Indipendencia. November 2nd is Day of the Dead, Dia de la los Muertos. November 20th is Revolution of Mexico, Dia de la Revolucion de Mexico.

December 12th is Virgin of Guadalupe, Dia de la Virgen de Guadalupe. December 25th is Christmas Day and the birth of God; Crismas y el Nacimiento del Nino Dias.

On December 31st, the end of the year, we make food. Family and friends come and enjoy it with us. First, we eat. After that we talk about the past and the news for next year. At midnight, each person takes twelve grapes and eats, but with each grape, we have to say a wish. The wishes are for the future like good health, more jobs, or get married next year. After that, we enjoy all night if it's possible; we dance, drink and give hugs for each person even the kids do the same like adults. We call to Mexico and say Happy New Year for all family and friends.

We like to follow the same traditions like we did in Mexico even if it's not the same here without family.

Maricela is 24 years old and is originally from Mexico.

The Red Envelope
Yan Kang, Lindstrom

The Chinese New Year is the biggest holiday in China; it is also called "The Spring Festival." On New Year's Eve, some people go out for dinner, and some cook at home. Everyone will be together for family reunions. They enjoy the good food and celebrating the coming New Year.

On the morning of New Year's Day, every child will put on new clothes. Parents give every child one red envelope with some money in it. They are wishing their child good luck in the New Year. The children are very happy after getting their envelope. They can buy some things they want with this money.

When the children turn eighteen years old, they can't get the red envelope with money anymore. I haven't had the envelope for a long, long time.

This year, God gave me the most precious gift, my daughter, Chyann, who came into the world on March 27th.

In February, the Chinese New Year will come. I'll prepare the red envelope for Chyann, and wish her good luck and happiness forever.

Yan Kang is 39 years old and is originally from Nanning, China.

Coffee Ceremony in Ethiopia
Fasika, Minnetonka

I would like to write about the Coffee Ceremony in my country. The Coffee Ceremony is one of the most recognizable parts of Ethiopian culture. Coffee is served when people come in your home on every holiday like New Year and when friends visit you. Coffee in Ethiopia is called Buna. The ceremony accompanies the serving of the coffee, which is sometimes served with Jebena, a clay coffee pot in which the coffee is boiled. I like coffee because coffee is originated from my country. I love the Coffee Ceremony too. Everybody gets together at Coffee Ceremony. I am very happy to be part of that culture.

New Year's Day in Vietnam
Trang Tran, Eagan

The lunar New Year's Day in 2009 was the last time I celebrated it in Vietnam. This important holiday is based on the lunar calendar and has many traditions. First, everyone cleans up their house, buys food and new clothes. The food for New Year's Day is very special. We buy four types of fruit and arrange it in a specific order: custard-apple, coconut, papaya and mango. There is a special meaning for this order. When you say the names of the fruit in Vietnamese, it sounds like words that mean people will have enough money in the next year. We also buy watermelon and special flowers. We make two kinds of sweet rice cakes. A round cake represents land. A square cake represents the sky.

Preparing for New Year's Day is busy. At midnight, many people crowd together and see the fireworks. New Year's Eve is happy. A three-day celebration begins on New Year's Day. People go to each other's houses and wish them a Happy New Year. The first day, we go to the grandparents' house. The second day we go to the other relatives' houses. The third day we go to the teacher's house and friends' houses. We eat so much, drink beer, play cards and talk together. It's very fun, happy, relaxing, and exciting!

One day, I'll go back to my country for the lunar New Year's Day.

Trang Tran is 22 years old and is originally from Vietnam.

Micaela Cedillo, Waite Park

I Am Thankful
Lucas Jiménez Dorantes, Minneapolis

I am thankful
I am thankful for my wife
I am thankful for my job
I am thankful for my children
I am thankful for weather
    Because she loves me
    Because I have too many foods
    Because they play in the house
    Because it is cold

Lucas Jiménez Dorantes is originally from Mexico.

CARNIVAL

I'm from Ecuador. It's a beautiful place with big mountains and small rivers. It's a green place. The main holiday in my country is Carnival. For Carnival, the people cook a lot and play together with water. The people play in the rivers. Sometimes people play with flour. They go dancing. I like Carnival.

Sandra Abad is from Ecuador. She has lived in Minnesota for three years and New York for four years before that. She lives in Apple Valley with her husband Juan and their two children. The rest of her family members are in Ecuador. She likes to read, go running, and cook. In the future, Sandra hopes to study psychology. Sandra is an ESL student at Grace Adult School in Apple Valley.

THE LOVE OF SOCCER

In Jamaica, soccer is the most popular sport. My uncle Mel and I love it with a passion. We both like to play it but we are not very good and that never stops us. I can still remember when I was growing up, every Sunday morning when everyone was getting ready to go to church, we would be trying to find a soccer game so we could play. We both dreamed of one day going to the World Cup of soccer to watch it played live. But we could never find the right time. Every four years when the World Cup games come around, we never have the time or the money. Like this time around, I have time, but he doesn't. There's always something stopping us from going together. So we are both going to do what we always do every four years when the games come around: watch it on television and make plans to go the next time around.

Bradley Clarke grew up in Jamaica and as an adult moved to Florida in 1997. He moved to Minnesota in October 2010 and lives in Minnetonka. He is now working towards completing his GED at Adult Options in Education, Hopkins.

♥Love is the base of every heart
Love is light in many days
yet why does it still fall apart
and feel love is dismay.

♥I've seen so much hope and joy
in the eyes of those around
what is that feeling by a boy.

♥Yet somenthing holds me back
a fear inside my heart.
A thing that I have lacked
through all my strange thoughts.

♥Thoughts of tears on my face
and broken heart to match
so I guard my heart in case
the disease of pain I catch.

♥I hide my feelings inside
so my heart won't be hurt
but even from what I hide
some lust in me still lurks.

★ alecksa gzz ★♥

Daniel Cantú, Owatonna

I Love Winter
Steve Olson, Edina

I love the shrill of tires squeaking across the packed snow
The tearing sound of a skate blade cutting into the ice
I love the silence of a fresh fallen snow
The tracks of all the critters laced across the landscape following
I love the smell of a warming wood fire pouring out of a chimney
The scent of a fresh cut Balsam, Cedar or Spruce
I love hearing hockey pucks bouncing off the boards of an outdoor rink
The slapping of sticks against the ice
I love the sound of alpine skis carving an arc into a loose top, hard packed snow
The trumpeting "whoo whoo" of winter swans singing their song, the rush of their long deliberate wing beat
I love the Budweiser commercials of regal and powerful Clydesdales drawing a sleigh
"Over the mountains and through the woods to Grandmother's house we go"
Over the stone bridge, winding through the snowy winter landscape to a fairy tale white colonial house ablaze with candles, only it is real
I love the twinkling lights on the trees of a downtown sidewalk
The decorative green wreaths hanging upon the lamp posts
I love the sound of a grouse flushing through the winter woods
And the snow that gently hits the forest floor following its departure
I love the sight of smoke escaping the top of a warming house
The clamor and cacophony of a ski chalet
I love the way big fluttering snowflakes float to the ground
And the way they melt to mist as they hit the warmth of my cheeks
I love the sound of a distant snow blower and the scraping of a shovel
Of hearty Minnesotans at work
I love the look of softly piled snow on the boughs of evergreens
And the deep periwinkle sky seen only in the late afternoon of winter
I love the pastel glow of a winter sunset
And the snow lightened sky of the night
I love the winter
And the wonderland of a changed season according to Mother Nature

Set Free, Goodbye to Thee
Tasha Moshier, Big Lake

It was one springtime day
I chose to walk away
I chose to believe
And to give up thee

I asked for forgiveness
And said a short prayer
I was saved
And my new life started there

Goodbye to Addiction
I have been set Free.
No longer can drugs and booze
Suck the life out of me.

I believe it was in these walls
That I learned how to be set free.
I believe it was in these walls
That made the addiction so clear to me.

It was this springtime day
I chose to walk away
While locked inside these walls
Of this lonely place called jail.

This place taught me to be
All the more that I have in me.
I have been set Free
And now I say, "Goodbye to Thee"

All About Me
Run Hussein, Minneapolis

Run
Short, smart, happy
Who likes warm weather in Somalia
Who is afraid of cockroaches
Who needs a husband in Kenya
Mother, wife, sister, student
Hussein

Run Hussein is originally from Somalia.

You've Got to Read This
Steven Pearson, Minneapolis

Some people say it's all on me
but when someone's missing some guidance
you're all they see
and it passes down through generations like
apples on a tree
With so many fathers not in the home
and mothers that can't do it on their own
it's going to take the neighborhood to do
something good
and start encouraging our little ones to do the
best that they could
They say there're three kinds of people in this
world
people that see what's going on
others that talk about what's going on
and people who act on what's going on.

And this last one is for everyone to take heed
"To Practice Makes Permanent not Perfect."

To the Great Spirit
Refugio Hernández-Muniz, Elk River

We are put in prison,
we are pushed hard, from all sides,
we are beaten down, we are bewildered,
but we don't lose hope.

They make us suffer,
but the Great Spirit doesn't desert us.
Locked down, knocked down, but not knocked out.
We are known, but we are unknowns.
We are dying, but we were not dead.
We are sad, but we're always glad.
We are poor, but we make people rich.
We have nothing but we own everything.

We are patient.

For you hold the weapons of the guidelines,
of the white man in your hands.
I have spoken freely.
With open heart, ears and eyes,
holding nothing back.
If the news of our sentences is good, or bad,
we won't be sad.

For our faith is true to you,
in our spiritual inner souls.

My Role Model
Kefaya Hassan, Brooklyn Park

He was the greatest person Allah created, and he still is the greatest human being. He was born on Monday, April 20 or 22 in Mecca in 571. He is our Prophet Mohammad (s.a.a.w). I love him more than myself. Not only me, but also all Muslims love him. He died more than 1,430 years ago but he lives in our hearts forever. He is the one who took us from the darkness to the light. He showed us the good way to live. He is my role model and our role model, and we remember him every day, all the time. I have more to say about my prophet. One paper is not enough. Every time when I pray, I ask Allah to make me his neighbor in heaven. Not only me, but all the people who believe in him. My Prophet, we love you and we miss you a lot.

A Holiday I Remember
Astrid Mamona, Saint Cloud

Last January 1st 2009, I received my Ivory Coast friends, Amy and her daughter Larissa. They were themselves at home, because her husband traveled to French Guyana where he was working. We invited them to come and take part at the feast with us that day. They came on the evening of the 31st—we were dancing all night together. On January 1st, we began to have breakfast. After that, we cooked a lot of food like salt fishes, vegetables, Italian food (Lasagna), etc.

That day, we had a lot of food to eat; we ate and ate a lot. After eating, we returned to dancing and drinking non-alcoholic beer and soft drinks, telling stories, giving advice, and making plans for the New Year. We were together through midnight. It was a very nice day; I would like another day like that one.

But, I remember also that my husband's friend, Claver, came with a gift (a car) for my son. He took it and began to move it. After a couple minutes, he destroyed it immediately. It was very hard for him to see the gift destroyed the moment he gave it to him. We were so sorry.

Astrid Mamona is originally from the Democratic Republic of Congo.

My History
MCA, Saint Louis Park

I remember Christmas of 1997. My family and I were celebrating Christmas, and we all were in my house. I can still remember the laughing faces of all. Everyone was having dinner and dancing, but something was not right. Among all this happiness, I had a bad feeling, and I started to feel sad. I knew I had to enjoy these moments most, because we seldom had the chance to see all my family together, and it was true. At that time, my family started to disintegrate. Today, I can't stop thinking about the day that we can gather and all look like that. Now almost all my family members are still missing. I try for complete happiness now.

Wilma Griebel, Southern Minnesota

Index of Authors

A

Sandra Abad 146
Andrei Abayeu 115
Shukri Abayle 110
Amina Abdi 1
Hajia Abdi 29
Kadar Abdi 113
Abdikarim 45
Lukman Abdile 35
Ahmed Abdullahi 104
Fatuma Abdullahi 28
Saeed Abdulle 75
Melese Abebe 79
Shamso Abshir 108
Khadija Adan 62
Abdinasir Aden 13
Fadumo Aden 31
Hassan A. Aden 102
Leyla Aden 19
Sewanta Adhikari 61
Denise Agbenowossi 10
Raad A. Ahmad 93, 111
Qalbinur Ahmed 89
Ayawavi Akpaglo 23
Al-Azzawi 141
Fadumo Ali 56, 59
Hadi Ali 110
Hussein Ali 53
Mohamed Abukar Ali 137
Sharifo Ali 96
Shukri Ali 72
Maliya Aliy 135
Dede Amagli 139
Amin 43
Zack Anderson 83
Andja 3
Anonymous 3, 8, 9, 17, 22, 24, 30, 34, 39, 42, 43, 49, 61, 66, 79, 80, 84, 95, 97, 104, 121, 125, 127, 129, 131, 136
AP 79
Arlan Arnold 143
Abdirisak Asad 121
Khadra Askar 137

B

Kadiatu Bah 95
Michael Bailor 65
Emily Balderas 29
Levoy Ballard iv
Diane Moss Baptiste 111
Sade Bausley 92
Miguel Angel Bautista 74
James Becerra 118
Begeh 85
David Boggie 11
J. R. Boswell 73
Armando Bryant 94
Hassan Budeye 37
Jerome Burks 117
Marites Burnett 112
María Bustillos 36

C

Daniel Cantú 147
Martha Carbajal 133
James Lee Carmichael 92
Micaela Cedillo 145
Johan Cerra 17
Chaly 106
Taeng Chamlongsong 4
Ia Chang 138
Jua Chang 120
Davone Chanthavongsa 127
Hui Ying Chen 55
Daopeth Cida 103
Bradley Clarke 146
Claudy 52
Hafida Colley 107
Manuel Contreras 59
Maricela Coronado 144
José Angel Cortez 101
Kay Cox 60
Alvaro Cruz 85
Angel Cruz 85
Mauricio Cruz 89

D

Igor Dadashev 87
Nadifo Dahir 2
Jaime R. Dejesus 39
Bhagirath Dhungana 28
Adam Dhunkal 20
Damon Dickerson 38
Hang Dinh 105
Garnary Doe 55
Nyanchew Donis 49
Mrs. Big Dottie 105
Heather Duong 111

E

Isir Egeh 27
Donald Egge 31
Wah Eh 13
Tiffany Eidum 3
Alfred Einberger 116
EJ 63
E.L. i, 34
Bernardino Enríquez 12
Chad Erickson 37
Faviola Estrada 115
Rocio Estrada 39
Lonnie Eubanks 71

F

Abdullahi Farah 19
Ali Farah 138
Deka Farah 82
Fasika 145
Kayoua Faust 56
FB 27
Starlin Fernández 119
Ariane Ferreira 65
Ahmed Firin 77
Marian Firin 22
Laura Flores 37
Wesley Fontes 80
Brenda Franco 20

G

A.G. 33
Daniel García 74
Virginia García Jiménez 70

Bill Gaskin 17
Gadeise Gebywe 72
Tshibola Gemaine 32
Aregash Gemedi 15
Hanifa Ghedi 25
Gabin Gitangwa 123
Marie Edoh Gnronfoun 33
Adán Gonzales 140
Shelly Gordien 103
Wilma Griebel 3, 4, 37, 47, 68, 150, Back cover
María Guaman 90
Suzy Guerra 70
Mostafa Guure 2

H

Iliana H. 123
Christina Hae 120
Qali Haji 135
Vang Hang 14
Paul Christopher Hanninen 63
Seila Has 41
Ahmed Hassan 129
Johara Hassan 91
Kefaya Hassan 150
Mahmood Hassan 139
Maryan Hassan 2
Houda Hazzaf 142
Sokunthea Hean 20
Cher Her 51
Da Her 104, 108
Mee Her 137
Toua Her 19
Nancy Hernández 143
Refugio Hernández-Muniz Front cover, 149
Angel Herrera 30
Abdullahi Hersi 20
Hijazi 142
Fatuma Hirsi 15
Vita Hladun 69
Chan Hou 10
Junjie Huang 83
Tim Hubble 124
Run Hussein 149

I

Sadia I. 12
Naji Ibrahim 16
Florence Iketalu 115
Isabel 75
Felipa Islas 93

J

Chavelle Jackson 86
Jennifer Jackson 101
Marisela Jaimes 106
Hawo Jama 41
Mukhtar A Jimaleh 47
Virginia García Jiménez 70
Lucas Jiménez Dorantes 145
Rebecca Jock 58
Lidia L. Juárez 25
Judith 142

K

Lillie K. 45
Yan Kang 144
Soukpaseut Keomany 47
Yenanesh Keryo 114
Zalina Khan 76
Ka Khang 1
Nhialue Khang 7
Kemsrean Kheng 48
Anna Kim 138
Keith Kinning 128
Mary Kitila 36
Gilford Knutson 1
Jayson Knutson 63, 87, 131
Elizabeth Kong 105
Aung Kyaing 7

L

E.L. i, 34
Jorge L 130
Cenovia Lagunas 12
DeShun Langley 119
Ho Chee Lau 82
Remeriza Laurie 132
Ngae Lay 90
Rosa Lazaro 4
Hong Le 18

Long Le 99
Van Le 7
German Lema 132
Daniel Lemu 8
Inna Leontyev 140
Akwata Lero 62
Brittany Lero 97
Charlene Litchke 53
Feicui Liu 21
Marilyn Lodermeier 114
Nhia Lor 5
Pa Lor 13
Nay Lorbliayao 90
Hui Luo 14
Toan Ly 136

M

Yassamin M. 94
Luci Magalhaes 141
Aisha Adam Mahmoud 22
Joaquín Maldonado 139
Astrid Mamona 150
Marcia 72
Marco 95
Silvia Martínez 28
Daring E. Martínez-Meza 123
MCA 150
Sandra McGraw 81
Lourdes Mendoza 73
Manuel Mendoza 70
Asha Mohamed 76
Safiyo Mohamed 54
Shamso Mohamed 113
Ayan Mohammed 100
Zahra Mohammed 21
Alvester Morman 64
Tasha Moshier 148
Sao Moua 69
Samira Mudey 2
María Murray 100
Abdulkadir Mursal 129
Mustafa Mussa 122

N

Shukri Naghiye 31
Thomas Nelson 88
Nereo 84

Dung Nguyen 125
Hoang Nguyen 40, 41
Kim Nguyen 2
Long Nguyen 124
Nghiem Nguyen 112
Phong PH Nguyen 25
Sima Noroozi 26

O

María Ochoa 94
Akoua Ofridam 131
Oleg 78
Ahmed Olol 45
Steve Olson 148
Halima Omar 42
Hassan Omar 27
Mary Ommundson 46
Orathai (Wai) 13
Maandeeq Osman 119

P

Shane Paige 116
Mariana Pallazhco 46
Yosef Baji Patrick 60
Wah Ka Paw Do Mu 122
Steven Pearson 149
Noe Pérez 100
Ngan Pham 46
Chanrithy Phoung 3
Margarita Polyakova 142
Samuel L Porter 67
Cinzia Pucciani 126

Q

Claudia Quevedo 81

R

Iryna Rabushka 24
Rachel 91
Anita Radnuz 82
Abshiro Rage 23
Araceli Ramírez 87
Colleen Reinke 108
Arcelia Reyes 44
Randall Ringo vi
Verónica River-Arteaga 98

Hawa Roba 36
Omar Roble 23
Carmen C. Rodríguez 98
Janette Rojas 75
Har Rom 58
Rosa Rome 141
April Romero 102
Victor R. Rosas 72

S

E.S.J. 101
Amina Sahal 121
Faduma Said 89
Fawsiyo Said 69
Antonieta Sánchez 36
Isabel Sánchez 89
Rene Manuel Sánchez Sr. 67
Ana Santos 53
Johnathan Saw 30
Eang Say 71
Bounhom Sayachack 44
Dan Selberg 76
Ilavarasi Selvam 77
Erika Serrano 56
Gustav K. Shackelton 70
Sabaha Sharif 109
Abeba Shashego 51
Farkhanda Sikandar 50
Siriporn 78
Barb Smead 72
Jonathon Smith 11
Levi Smith 113
Robert A. Smith 15
Jacob Solberg 65
Lirouwane Sow 32
Joni G Sperandio 81
Clarita Stiles 107
Fadumo Sulub 112
Kevin L Sund 134

T

Sabina Tabukum 98
Bahtiraj Tahir 71
Miguel Tamayo 97
Junru Tang 90
Weynshet Tesfaye 35
Hlee Thao 58

Index of Authors - 153

Pa Houa Thao 71
Soua Thao 9
Truc Mai Tran Thi 33
Janice Thompson 99
John Thurston 38
Carrie Thyes-Brown 102
Fauzia Shawich Tia 61
Lorenzo Torregrossa 35
Tou Vang Lee 50
Trang Tran 145
Luta Tshihamba 29

V

Vadim 18
Bla Vang 60
Houa Vang 121
Kao Vang 110
Mai Vang 113
Neng Vang 43
Pang Vang 6
Vani 26
Eliud Velázquez 128
VG 128
Tao Vue 7, 139

W

Samson Waddell 63
Kamella Wahidi 82
Melaka Walton 108
Mohamed-Deq Warsame 91
Mohamed Warsame 11
Wesley Watts 65
Daniel Weston 28
Carrie White 9
Nick Whitman 67
Elliott Williams 66
James Williams 52
Kendall Williams 73
Roman Worku 55

X

Mai Lia Xiong 24
Nan Xiao 130

Y

Diane Yanacheak 119
Der Yang 140
Houa Yang 117
Melia Yang 12
MorMai Yang 110
Nhia Doua Yang 38
Yia Yang 116
Deqo Yasin 34
Keith June Year 63
See Yee 103
Yellow Leaf 39
Yurub Yusuf 49

Z

Zareen Zafar 57
Israel Zamorano 15
Yuanbin Zhang 1
Miao Zhen 85
Yong Hong Zhu 18
Jian Zou 21
María Mercedes Zumarraga 137